Three Spa␣

M000284924

The Duchess ␣␣ ␣␣␣␣␣␣ ␣ ␣␣␣␣␣␣ ␣
The Capulets and Montagues
by Lope de Vega

Cleopatra
by Rojas Zorrilla

Lope de Vega and Rojas Zorrilla were two of the most famous
and successful playwrights of the Spanish Golden Age. From
their prodigious output, the three plays in this volume, based on
similar sources to Shakespeare's and Webster's versions, provide
a fascinating comparison with their English counterparts.

Lope Félix de Vega Carpio, born in Madrid in 1562, two
years before Shakespeare, was something of a child prodigy.
Writing for the public theatres from his early twenties, he gave
the plays their definitive three-act form, and in the course of his
career as a dramatist was said to have written 1,800 secular and
400 religious works, including *Fuente Ovejuna, Peribáñez, The Knight
from Olmedo, Punishment Without Revenge*, and *The Dog in the Manger.*
His productivity as a writer was equalled only by the energy of
his love life, for he was twice married and had numerous love-
affairs, even after he took Holy Orders at the age of fifty-two.
Not without cause was he known in his time – at least as far as
his writing was concerned – as a 'monster of Nature'.

Francisco de Rojas Zorrilla, unlike Lope de Vega, wrote
mainly for the court theatres. Born in Toledo in 1607, when
Lope was forty-five and at the height of his career, Rojas
subsequently spent most of his life in Madrid, and by his mid-
twenties had already gained a reputation as a dramatist. In 1635
seven of his plays were performed at the Royal Palace, and in
1640 his version of the Romeo-and-Juliet story, *The Factions in
Verona*, was commissioned to open the magnificent new court
theatre in the grounds of the Buen Retiro, Madrid's royal park.
Rojas was particularly known for his tragedies, of which *None
Below the King* is a good example. His prickly character often
created enemies in literary and court circles, and his death in
1648 at the age of only forty-one may have been the result of
foul play.

Bloomsbury Methuen drama anthologies include

Contemporary African Plays
(Wole Soyinka, *Death and the King's Horseman*; Percy Mtwa, Mbongeni Ngema and Barney Simon, *Woza Albert!*; Ama Ata Aidoo, *Anowa*; Femi Osofisan, *The Chattering and the Song*; Andrew Whaley, *The Rise and Shine of Comrade Fiasco*; Alemseged Tesfai, *The Other War*)

Contemporary Australian Plays
(Hannie Rayson, *Hotel Sorento*; David Williamson, *Dead White Males*; Ron Elisha, *Two*; Wesley Enoch and Deborah Mailman, *The Seven Stages of Grieving*; Keith Robinson and Tony Taylor, *The Popular Mechanicals*)

Modern Catalan Plays
(Joan Brossa, *The Quarrelsome Party*; Rodolf Sirera, *The Audition*; Josep Maria Benet i Jornet, *Desire*; Sergi Belbel, *Fourplay*)

Far From the Land: Contemporary Irish Plays
(Vincent Woods, *At the Black Pig's Dyke*; Daragh Carville, *Language Roulette*; Enda Walsh, *Disco Pigs*; Donal O'Kelly, *Bat the Father, Rabbit the Son*; Patrick McCabe, *Frank Pig Says Hello*; Conall Morrison, *Hard to Believe*)

Frontline Drama 6: New French Plays
(Christophe Pellet, *One More Wasted Year*; Noëlle Renaude, *The Northern Fox*; Catherine Anne, *Agnès*; Natacha de Pontcharra, *Mickey the Torch*; Xavier Durringer, *A Desire to Kill on the Tip of the Tongue*)

Six Greek Comedies
(Aristophanes, *Birds, Frogs, Women in Power*; Menander, *The Woman from Samos*; Euripides, *Cyclops, Alkestis*)

Six Greek Tragedies
(Aeschylus, *Persians, Prometheus Bound*; Sophocles, *Women of Trachis, Philoctetes*; Euripides, *Trojan Women, Bacchae*)

Four Roman Comedies
(Plautus, *Mostellaria (The Haunted House), Casina (A Funny Thing Happened on the Way to the Wedding)*; Terence, *The Eunuch, Brothers*)

The Methuen Book of Contemporary Latin American Plays
Mario Vargas Llosa, *La Chunga*; Egon Wolff, *Paper Flowers*; José Triana, *Medea in the Mirror*)

Live Theatre: Six Plays from the North East
(Tom Hadaway, *The Filleting Machine*; C.P. Taylor, *You Are My Heart's Delight*; Alan Plater, *Shooting the Legend*; Lee Hall, *Wittgenstein on Tyne*; Sean O'Brien, *Laughter When We're Dead*; Julia Darling, *Cold Calling*)

Made in Scotland
(Mike Cullen, *The Cut*; Simon Donald, *The Life of Stuff*; Sue Glover, *Bondagers*; Duncan McLean, *Julie Allardyce*)

Three Spanish Golden Age Plays

The Duchess of Amalfi's Steward
The Capulets and Montagues
by Lope de Vega

Cleopatra
by Rojas Zorrilla

*translated and
introduced by Gwynne Edwards*

B L O O M S B U R Y
LONDON · NEW DELHI · NEW YORK · SYDNEY

Bloomsbury Methuen Drama

An imprint of Bloomsbury Publishing Plc

50 Bedford Square	1385 Broadway
London	New York
WC1B 3DP	NY 10018
UK	USA

www.bloomsbury.com

Bloomsbury is a registered trade mark of Bloomsbury Publishing Plc

The collection first published in the United Kingdom in 2005 by
Methuen Publishing Limited

These translations first published 2005
© 2005 by Gwynne Edwards

Collection and introduction © 2005 by Gwynne Edwards

Gwynne Edwards has asserted his right under the Copyright, Designs and
Patents Act, 1988, to be identified as author of this work.

Visit www.bloomsbury.com to find out more about our authors and their books
You will find extracts, author interviews, author events and you can sign up for
newsletters to be the first to hear about our latest releases and special offers.

British Library Cataloguing-in-Publication Data
A catalogue record for this book is available from the British Library.

ISBN: PB: 978-0-4137-7475-0
       EPDF: 978-1-4081-5042-9
       EPUB: 978-1-4081-5041-2

Library of Congress Cataloging-in-Publication Data
A catalog record for this book is available from the Library of Congress.

Contents

For Sarah

Chronology

Introduction

Shakespeare's *Antony and Cleopatra* and *Romeo and Juliet*, and Webster's *The Duchess of Malfi*, are among the best-known and often-performed plays in English theatre. In comparison, Lope de Vega's *The Duchess of Amalfi's Steward* (*El mayordomo de la duquesa de Amalfi*) and *The Capulets and Montagues* (*Castalvines y Monteses*), and Rojas Zorrilla's *Cleopatra* (*Los áspides de Cleopatra*), have never achieved the same degree of success or popularity in Spain. Such neglect is surprising, given the stature and importance of Lope in particular and the attractive and familiar nature of all three subjects, but the explanation probably lies in the fact that both Lope and Rojas were such extremely productive playwrights – Lope more so than Rojas – that much of their work has been neglected, and undue emphasis has been and continues to be placed on a mere handful of plays, of which Lope's *Fuente Ovejuna* and Rojas' *None Below the King* are examples. In their time, however, Lope and Rojas were quite as famous and as successful in the theatre as Shakespeare and Webster, and the stories which they dramatised in the plays in question were well known throughout western Europe, not least through the short stories of Mateo Bandello and the translations and adaptations of his work into English, French, and Spanish. The Spanish dramatists' handling of their source material was, as we shall see, often very different from that of their English counterparts, and allows for a fascinating comparison of their respective personalities, their dramatic methods, and the nature of the theatre for which they wrote their plays. The fact that the Spanish plays are less well known than their English equivalents does not mean, furthermore, that they are inferior in quality. These translations will, hopefully, reveal their merits, make for fruitful comparisons, and create a greater interest in the theatre of Spain's Golden Age, which, in its richness and vitality, is certainly a worthy rival to its English counterpart.

Lope de Vega

Lope Félix de Vega Carpio, widely acclaimed as one of Spain's truly great dramatists both in his own time and afterwards, was born in Madrid on 25 November 1562, two years before Shakespeare. He was the son of what we would now describe as a middle-class family which originally came from the area around Santander in the north of Spain. Lope's father, Felices de Vega Carpio, was a man of strong religious tendencies who, accompanied by his children, regularly attended to the sick, carrying out the most menial tasks at one of the Madrid hospitals. Lope seems to have inherited his father's religious streak, but he was also an impulsive boy who, at the age of twelve or thirteen, ran away with a friend. This impetuous aspect of his character would manifest itself in the years ahead, both in the numerous scrapes and difficulties in which he became embroiled, and in the various love-affairs which dominated his adult life. From an early age, Lope also displayed notable literary gifts: he is said to have been composing verses at the age of five and to have written his first play at the age of twelve. His early education was at a Jesuit school in Madrid, from which he proceeded to the University of Alcalá de Henares where he studied until the age of twenty. He was evidently a young man of great intelligence, highly gifted in mathematics and languages. He was able to write in Latin and had a thorough knowledge of Italian.

At the age of twenty-one, Lope embarked on a love-affair with Elena Osorio, the daughter of a celebrated actor-manager for whom he had agreed to write plays. Elena was already married, but neither her husband nor her father appears to have raised serious objections to her liaison with Lope over a period of four years. But when, in 1587, it became clear that she had turned her attentions to another man, Lope's sense of betrayal was such that he launched a series of bitter attacks against Elena and her family, in which he described her as a prostitute and her family as living off her ill-gotten gains. It landed Lope in court, where he was tried for and found guilty of libel. He was therefore banished from Madrid for eight years and from Castile for

two. He moved to Valencia, but a few months later he was
back in Madrid, attempting to elope with Isabel de Urbina,
daughter of the King-at-Arms to Philip II. Initially objecting
to their daughter's marriage to someone they regarded as
her social inferior – as well as to his criminal record –
Isabel's parents eventually consented to her marriage by
proxy after Lope had left Madrid and returned to Valencia.
Shortly afterwards, in 1588, he and his brother joined the
San Juan, a ship which formed part of the Armada and
which was soon to set out from Lisbon in order to unseat
Queen Elizabeth I.

Having survived what proved to be a disaster for the
Spanish fleet, Lope returned to Valencia and, when his two-
year banishment from Castile had ended, moved to Toledo
and then to Alba de Torres, near Salamanca, where he was
employed in the service of the Duke of Alba. In 1595 his
wife died, and Lope embarked on a series of amorous
relationships. His involvement with Antonia Trillo de
Armento in 1596 led to criminal charges and another
appearance in a court of law. Two years later, he married
Juana de Guarda, the daughter of a wealthy Madrid
butcher, but this did not prevent him from having an affair
with the well-known actress, Micaela de Luján, when her
husband was out of the country. The relationship lasted
some eight years and produced several children.

In need of money to support his dependants, as well as his
children by more than one woman, Lope combined his
writing for the stage with secretarial duties on behalf of the
Duke of Sessa, who became his patron in 1605. Sharing the
young Duke's addiction to women, Lope is known to have
written his employer's love-letters for many years. In 1614,
after the death of his second wife, Juana, Lope took Holy
Orders at the age of fifty-two, but this in no way inhibited
his taste for women, for in 1615 he began an affair with a
married woman, Marta de Nevares Santoyo, and took her
to live with him. The relationship lasted for some years, but
by 1628 Marta had become blind and subsequently became
insane. She died in 1632, leaving Lope, at seventy years of
age, to look after their sixteen-year-old daughter, Antonia.

In an act that ironically paralleled her father's amorous
activities, Antonia ran off with a young courtier in 1634,
and the same year saw Lope's son, also called Lope, killed in
a naval engagement in the Caribbean. Clearly saddened by
these events, Lope died on 27 August 1635 at the age of
seventy-three.

While the events of his private life were extremely
colourful and tempestuous, Lope's career as a dramatist was
equally exciting. Described by Cervantes as a 'monster of
Nature' on account of his prolific output, Lope's
contemporary, Juan Pérez de Montalbán, attributed to him
1,800 secular and 400 religious plays. Of the secular plays,
around 400 remain, roughly ten times the number written
by Shakespeare. Acclaimed by a theatre-going public
possessing a voracious appetite for new plays, Lope's boast
of turning out a play a day was doubtless exaggerated, but
his output certainly points to his popularity. The phrase 'It's
by Lope' ('Es de Lope') is an indication of the irresistible
appeal his work had for a contemporary audience. He was,
in effect, the star of the new writing of his day.

Rojas Zorrilla
Francisco de Rojas Zorrilla was born in Toledo on 4
October 1607, when Lope de Vega was forty-five years old
and an experienced and successful dramatist. In
comparison, Rojas is less well known than Lope, but he was,
as we shall see, both famous and successful in his own time,
the equivalent, perhaps, of Webster to Shakespeare. He was
the eldest of the six children of Francisco Pérez de Rojas, a
naval officer, and Doña Mariana de Vesga y Zorrilla. When
Rojas was three years old, the family moved to Madrid,
where his father entered the service of the Marqués de
Loriana, and where, growing up in a house in the Plaza del
Angel, close to the area where Cervantes and Lope de Vega
had their homes, and close too to the important theatres,
the Corral de la Cruz and the Corral del Príncipe, the
young Rojas' interest in the stage was evidently stimulated.
He probably received his university education at the

prestigious University of Salamanca, after which he
returned to Madrid and concentrated on writing for the
theatre. By 1632, when he was twenty-five, he had already
gained a reputation as a dramatist, particularly a court
dramatist, and was described by his contemporary, Juan
Pérez de Montalbán, as a 'bold, assured and exciting poet,
as praise for his brilliant plays suggests'. Indeed, even at the
beginning of his career he was collaborating with the most
successful dramatists of his day, including Calderón, Luis
Vélez de Guevara, Pérez de Montalbán, and Antonio
Coello. It would not be long before he was challenging the
pre-eminence of Calderón in both the public and the court
theatres.

Rojas' adaptation for the stage of Cervantes's Byzantine
novel *Persiles and Segismunda* had made a strong impression
on the king, Philip IV, when it was performed in 1633 at
El Pardo, one of the royal residences outside Madrid.
Consequently, Rojas became well established as a court
dramatist, and in 1635 seven of his plays were performed at
the Royal Palace in Madrid. Despite this success, however,
his independence of mind and his sharp wit often created
problems for him. In 1638, for example, a poetic
entertainment was held at court in which Rojas amusingly
lampooned a number of court poets. Shortly afterwards, it
was reported that he had been murdered by those he had
offended. Although the report was exaggerated, the fact that
Rojas was attacked and badly injured is proof enough of the
bitter rivalry which often existed at that time between
writers and their supporters.

The year 1640 proved to be a significant one. On 4
February Rojas achieved a considerable theatrical success
when his Romeo and Juliet play, *The Factions in Verona*, was
commissioned to open the magnificent new court theatre, El
Coliseo, in the grounds of the Buen Retiro on the eastern
outskirts of Madrid. The same year also saw the publication
of the first volume of his plays, all of which had been staged.
And on 21 November Rojas married Doña Catalina Yáñez
Trillo de Mendoza, by whom he had a son a year later.
Prior to this, in 1636, an affair with a married actress, María

de Escobedo, had produced a daughter – evidence of the relaxed moral standards which prevailed in the theatre profession, though Rojas does not appear to have been as great a womaniser as Lope de Vega.

Little is known about the performance of Rojas' plays over the next four years, though it seems likely that he continued writing. But in the autumn of 1644, theatre activity in Spain suffered a serious setback. Firstly, those who objected to the immorality of the theatre in general had succeeded, earlier in the year, in obtaining a ban against all but historical and religious plays. And secondly, the death of the queen, Isabel, in October, brought about the suspension of all public performances. Two years later the death of Prince Baltasar Carlos closed the theatres until 1649. It was a series of events which effectively marked the end of Rojas' career as a dramatist.

During these years of theatrical inactivity, Rojas published at his own expense the second volume of his plays. In 1643 moreover, Philip IV, in recognition of Rojas' services to court theatre, had nominated him for membership of the Order of Santiago, an enormous honour and privilege at that time. Acceptance into the Order required, however, exhaustive investigation into the nominee's family background in order to ensure that it was not tainted by Moorish or Jewish blood – both the Moors and the Jews had previously been expelled from Spain. The resulting report suggested not only that Rojas had both Moorish and Jewish ancestors, some of whom had fallen foul of the Inquisition, but that he had even bribed witnesses to conceal these facts. It was a damning indictment, but one which, with the support of influential individuals at court, Rojas finally succeeded in overcoming in 1645.

He was to write only one more play, an *auto sacramental* or religious play called *The Great Courtyard of the Palace*, which was performed during the Corpus Christi celebrations in Madrid in 1647. By this time he seemed to have lost his touch, for *The Great Courtyard* is a decidedly inferior piece. Rojas died on 23 January 1648 at the age of forty-one, possibly the victim of foul play.

In contrast to Lope de Vega, Rojas enjoyed a relatively short career as a writer, for the closure of the theatres and his early death meant that it lasted for little more than a dozen years. Even so, between forty and fifty authentic plays survive, evidence enough of both the demand for his work and of his commitment to the theatre. Moreover, his collaboration with such significant dramatists as Calderón and his popularity·with Philip IV in particular, point to his status in the theatrical world of his time.

Drama in the Spanish Golden Age
The secular drama of Spain's Golden Age had its origins in the work of a number of significant writers between 1490 and 1580, among whom Juan del Encina (1468?–1530?), Gil Vicente (1465?–1536?), and Bartolomé de Torres Naharro (1485?–1520?) are generally considered to be the initiators. Dividing his time between Spain and Italy, Encina wrote fourteen *églogas* (eclogues), essentially verse dialogues between shepherds and other rustic characters, which contain both broad humour and sophistication, and which, above all, contributed substantially to the importance of the comic rustic in the later drama. Gil Vicente, more important and gifted than Encina, was the author of forty-four plays written, like those of his contemporary, for a select, private audience, but ranging from short sketches to devotional pieces, morality plays, farces, and romantic comedies, all of them revealing technical skill, a gift for dialogue, an aptitude for comedy, and a feeling for poetry. Even so, the work of both writers lacks the sense of stage action which we now demand as an essential requisite in theatre, and which distinguishes the plays of Torres Naharro, the third and most influential member of this group. Based in Rome and Naples for most of his creative life – his plays were published if not performed in Spain – he wrote for a much more varied audience than did Encina or Vicente, both of whom catered for aristocrats and/or ecclesiasts. Embracing low-life comedies of manners and romantic intrigues, his work reveals a new complexity of

plot, a predilection for certain themes – the importance of honour, the conflict between love and social position – and the mixing of the serious and the comic, all of which would become characteristic features of the later Spanish drama.

Another significant step forward concerned the formation in the 1540s and 1550s of acting companies performing plays for the general public and led by an actor-manager who was also quite often a playwright. The most important and best-known of these was Lope de Rueda (1509?–65), who, though based from 1552 in Valladolid, travelled widely throughout Spain, performing religious and secular plays. Praised by Cervantes, who saw him perform, Rueda was also the author of five full-length plays, five colloquies, and a dozen or so short comic pieces known as *pasos*. Marked by their broad humour, lively action, and vibrant characters, the *pasos* in particular look forward to the later drama, but Rueda's importance lay less in his ability as a dramatist than in his efforts to entertain a broad and varied audience and, by so doing, to create the foundations for a popular theatre. This process was further encouraged from the late 1540s by the arrival in Spain of Italian theatre companies whose presence until the end of the century seems to have led to the setting up of the first permanent theatre buildings in the late 1570s. This in turn inspired Spanish companies to follow their example.

Along with Lope de Rueda, Juan de la Cueva (1550?–1610?) should also be regarded as one of the most influential dramatists of his day. By no means a brilliant playwright, he was a theorist and an innovator who, in mixing the serious and the comic, breaking the classical unity of time, and employing different metres for particular situations, clearly set the scene for the more radical dramatic experiments of Lope de Vega and his contemporaries and successors. In addition, important changes were introduced by those dramatists who, in the second half of the sixteenth century, sought to write classical tragedy in Spanish: Jerónimo Bermúdez (1530?–99), Andrés Rey de Artieda (1544–1613), Cristóbal de Virués (1550–1609), Lupercio Leonardo de Argensola (1550–1613),

and Gabriel Lasso de la Vega (1569–1623?). Although the
theatre-going public did not take to their plays, each of these
dramatists influenced in some way the course of Spanish
theatre: reducing in number the five acts of classical tragedy,
eliminating the chorus, and dispensing with some of the
restrictions of the classical unities.

Last but not least, Miguel de Cervantes (1547–1616),
though eclipsed in popularity by Lope de Vega, made a
significant contribution to the Spanish stage. Closer to
writers like Virués in his neo-classical leanings, Cervantes
wrote one of the very best Spanish tragedies, *The Siege of
Numancia*, which is still often performed. On the other hand,
his later three-act plays and interludes were an attempt to
write in the manner of Lope de Vega, whose brilliance
Cervantes finally recognised after initial feelings of hostility.

Although some of the principal characteristics of the
secular drama of Spain's Golden Age had been created by
the dramatists mentioned above, they were consolidated
and further developed by Lope de Vega from about 1580.
In an influential poetic essay, *The New Art of Writing Plays*,
published in 1609, he set out the precepts which had already
dominated his work for the past quarter of a century. This
dramatic formula was, furthermore, taken up by all the
major dramatists who were his contemporaries or his
successors: Tirso de Molina (1581?–1648), Guillén de
Castro (1569–1631), Pérez de Montalbán (1602–38), Ruiz
de Alarcón (1581?–1639), Mira de Amescua (1574?–1644),
Luis Vélez de Guevara (1579–1644), Francisco de Rojas
Zorrilla (1607–48), and Calderón (1600–81). The format
was one which worked well in practice and has survived
until modern times, not least in the plays of Lorca. In terms
of structure, Lope perfected the play in three acts: the first
act sets out the situation, the second complicates it –
arriving at a critical juncture halfway through – and the
third resolves it, but without revealing the ending too early.
As well as being neat and well-proportioned, the play ran
for little more than two hours and did not, for that very
reason, unduly try the patience of a notoriously restless
Spanish audience.

Another significant aspect of Lope's approach to writing plays involved his rejection of classical rules, including the strict separation of serious and comic elements. In this respect the tragi-comic plays of the Golden Age clearly parallel their Elizabethan and Jacobean counterparts. In addition, as in Shakespearean drama, the action of plays was free-ranging and the time-scale flexible, in contrast to the classical rules governing the time and place of the stage-action. The basic principle behind Lope's beliefs was, as in the case of mixing the comic and the serious, that a play should be true to life, so the classical insistence on limiting the on-stage action to one location and to twenty-four hours was the complete opposite of that idea. On the other hand, the choice of verse over prose as the favoured means of expression appears to undermine the principle of verisimilitude since in the real world no one speaks in verse. Even so, the decision to write verse drama may be explained by the fact that verse was traditionally regarded as more pleasing to the ear than prose, and, in any case, was as much to the liking of Golden Age audiences as it was to the Elizabethans. At the same time, though, Lope and his followers made every effort to ensure that their characters spoke in the kind of language appropriate to their station in life: royalty in a weighty manner, lovers in a passionate and emotional way, servants in a down-to-earth and vigorous style. In addition, Lope advocated the use of particular stanza forms, ranging from three to ten lines (and sometimes a fourteen-line sonnet) for specific situations, and he favoured too the eight-syllable line, rather shorter and quicker when spoken than the Elizabethan line of ten or eleven syllables. The shorter line allowed the action of the play to proceed with the speed and vigour demanded by a Spanish audience.

Lope's aim, no less than Shakespeare's, was to entertain and please his audience, and, of course, to earn his living as a successful playwright. His secular plays therefore deal with subjects which had an appeal for contemporary audiences. Many are comedies set in the Spain of his day and in which the characters belong to the lower nobility. Others were based on particular events in Spanish history, of which the best-known is probably *Fuente Ovejuna*, set in the fifteenth century and in which the inhabitants of the town of that name rebel against and kill their abusive overlord. In addition, Lope often turned to the Bible for material which he knew would be of interest to his public. And he also wrote a number of powerful tragedies, some inspired by historical sources, and others, as in the case of *The Duchess of Amalfi's Steward* and *The Capulets and Montagues*, drawn from literary sources. Lope's range of subject matter was thus considerable, and in this respect he was followed by all his successors.

Although Lope wrote primarily for the public theatres, his plays were sometimes performed in the houses of the nobility, as well as in the much more sophisticated court theatres which, as we shall see, developed during the first quarter of the seventeenth century. In 1605, for example, *The Knight from Illescas* was performed in the presence of Philip III in the gardens of the house of his first minister, the powerful Duke of Lerma. In 1614 *Beauty's Prize* was presented in the open air at Lerma, where the sets which were built on the river banks included two mountains, a palace, a temple, and an enchanted castle. At one point a ship large enough to carry thirty people was required to founder on a rock in the river. And in 1622 an extremely lavish production of *The Golden Fleece* was staged at the royal palace in Aranjuez. Plays which were originally written for the court theatres would subsequently be presented in the public theatres in a much simpler form, while those which had been written specifically for the public theatres would often then receive a much more ambitious production at court.

Rojas Zorrilla, like his contemporaries, largely followed the dramatic principles established by Lope. Even so, by the time Rojas began his career as a dramatist, Spanish theatre had moved on from the innovatory and experimental stage represented by Lope to a period of consolidation, embodied above all in the careful and brilliant artistry of Calderón. In this respect, Rojas and his fellow dramatists produced work

distinguished by carefully constructed plots and, in
particular, by highly polished and sophisticated language in
which ornate imagery played an important part. At the
same time, Rojas was very much an individualist who
delighted in making fun of accepted social values and
particular dramatic conventions. In many of the so-called
'honour' plays of the period, notably those by Calderón, a
husband kills his wife, or her lover, or both, if an affair, or
even suspicion of an affair, threatens his good name. In *Each
to his Own*, on the other hand, Rojas turns the traditional
topic on its head by having the wife kill the lover when he
returns to pursue her, after which husband and wife settle
down happily. Again, while at the end of a play most
dramatists introduced a marriage or marriages to tie up
loose ends and suggest a final harmony, many of Rojas'
plays are distinguished by the absence of marriage. He
frequently undermined the drama's traditional concern with
questions of love and honour by mocking them, not least in
his sharp, biting, and irreverent comedies. But Rojas was
also attracted to tragic themes which ranged from Spanish
to classical subjects: in the former case, *None Below the King*,
in the latter, *Cleopatra*.

While Rojas largely established a reputation as a court
dramatist, he also saw many of his plays performed in the
public theatres. Lope, as we have seen, wrote mainly for the
latter, for at first they were the only form of theatre building
in existence. But by the time Rojas began writing plays in
the early 1630s, the public and court theatres existed side by
side, and it was therefore natural that he and his
contemporaries should see their plays performed in both.

The theatres
Of the three plays published here, *The Duchess of Amalfi's
Steward* and *The Capulets and Montagues* were written for and
performed in the public theatres or *corrales*, which, as the
word suggests, were large courtyards, and which came into
prominence in the last quarter of the sixteenth century.
Cleopatra may also have been performed in the public

theatres, though, on the whole, it seems particularly well
suited to a performance at court. As for the origins of the
corrales, there existed in Madrid in the last quarter of the
sixteenth century two charitable organisations – the
Cofradía de la Pasión y Sangre de Jesucristo and the
Cofradía de la Soledad de Nuestra Señora – which sought
to raise funds for their hospitals by obtaining from the local
authority permission to hire courtyards for the performance
of plays. In 1579 and 1582 respectively, two such *corrales*, the
Corral de la Cruz and the Corral del Príncipe, became the
focal points for the performance of plays in Madrid, and
they remained so throughout the seventeenth century. At
the same time, Toledo, Segovia, Valencia, Barcelona,
Zaragoza, and Seville also developed theatres of a similar
kind. Most of the great dramatists mentioned earlier
produced much of their work for the *corrales* and sought
thereby to win the approval of increasingly demanding
audiences. The competition was intense, public demand
insatiable, and the number of plays performed remarkable.

The *corrales* were rectangular in shape and surrounded by
houses of many storeys whose upper balconies and windows
looked down on the audience and the stage. The latter was
situated at one end of the courtyard, its apron projecting
into the auditorium and thus creating a sense of closeness
and intimacy with the audience. Both the apron and the
mid-stage were uncluttered areas, but the back-stage was
more complicated. The actors made their entrances and
exits through curtains or doors at either side of the back-
stage from the dressing-rooms situated nearby. In the
middle of the back-stage was a curtained area known as a
'discovery space', so called because its curtains could be
whipped back to reveal some startling sight, such as a
bloody corpse. Above this inner stage was a gallery which
could be used to enact balcony scenes and the like, while the
windows and balconies of the houses immediately behind
the stage could be utilised in the performance to represent
heaven, and the balconies could also be connected to the
stage by means of ladders. Access to the fires of hell was
provided by trapdoors in the stage itself and the stage could

also be linked by ramps to the area immediately in front of it, which was roped off from the audience and sometimes used for battle scenes or jousts, with real horses. Scenery in the *corrales* was, at least in the early days of their development, relatively simple, for the quick-moving action of Golden Age plays did not allow for complex scene changes. But, as the resources of the theatres became greater through the seventeenth century, more ambitious effects became possible, such as rocks opening up and revealing some amazing sight, or cloud machines descending from heaven and bearing angels. In contrast to the simplicity of the scenery, costumes were much more lavish. This would have been especially true of the royal and aristocratic characters of the plays published here: the Duchess of Amalfi, the Duke of Verona, and, of course, Cleopatra. This said, costumes were always contemporary, and no attempt was made to recreate a historical period.

The physical characteristics of the stage in the *corrales* were remarkably similar to their Elizabethan counterparts. The latter too had a large open acting area at the back of which was an inner stage. Above this there was a gallery which could be used in the action for scenes set on a higher level, such as an assault on the battlements of a castle. Scenery, as in the *corrales*, was relatively simple, much being left to the imagination of the audience as to where and when the on-stage events were taking place. On the other hand, the English playhouses were in general more sumptuous than their Spanish counterparts, and acting companies had a much more secure base in particular theatre buildings. The similarity between the development of the theatre in England and Spain does not mean, though, that one influenced the other; rather that, in both countries, that development was a response to similar circumstances and similar public demand.

In the *corrales* the stage and some rows of seats at the side and back of the auditorium were covered, but most of the latter was open to the elements. This meant, of course, that the performance of plays took place only in favourable weather. And because neither the stage nor the auditorium enjoyed the benefits of lighting, plays were performed in the afternoon. When, therefore, scenes in a play took place at night, the audience was obliged to use its imagination, for the actors on stage might well be bathed in sunlight. Indications of the time of day or night when particular events in a play occurred were to be found in the text, which acted as a kind of guide to the audience, and the same was true of changes of location.

As for the physical layout of the auditorium, most of the audience stood in the area immediately in front of the stage and was composed of commoners, some of whom were the equivalent of the Elizabethan 'groundlings'. They were often unruly and had little hesitation in expressing their dissatisfaction with what they were seeing, be it with whistles, rattles, or rotten fruit. To the sides and back of this standing area were tiered rows of benches known as *gradas*, which were more expensive and would therefore contain the better-off elements of the audience. In the auditorium itself, poorer women were confined to an area known as the *cazuela* or 'stew-pan'. The windows and balconies of the houses to the sides of the auditorium were the equivalent of the boxes in later theatre buildings and, known as the *aposentos*, could be hired by the nobility for the theatre season. Separate entrances for men and women were at the back of the auditorium. After the payment of an entrance fee, individuals then paid an extra charge for admission to different parts of the theatre.

Acting companies were run by a manager who, despite being called an *autor*, was not necessarily a writer. A typical company consisted of around fourteen actors: four young men, including the leading man; six women; two men who specialised in playing elderly roles; and two who specialised in comic parts. As for the women, they were allotted specific roles, be it first, second, third, or fourth *dama*, the *autor*'s wife often being the leading lady. Plays were obtained directly from dramatists, who often lost control of their material, or existing texts were used. Because of the huge demand for new plays, productions usually ran for no more than two or three days. One important difference between English and

Spanish acting companies lay in the presence in the latter of a significant number of actresses. Female roles in the plays of Elizabethan and Jacobean dramatists were played by boy actors or young men who were extremely skilled in this respect, and the roles of the Duchess of Malfi, Juliet, and Cleopatra would have been performed by a male attempting to create the illusion of being a female. As the composition of Spanish companies indicates, there was no such restriction concerning females on the stage, despite the often dissolute nature of their private activities and the pressures imposed in many areas of life by a strict Catholic Church. Actresses were required by law to be married and no unmarried women, including widows, were allowed to act. Consequently, marriages in the theatre profession were frequently based not on love but on economic and professional considerations, and many actresses who were suddenly widowed quickly remarried in order to be able to continue in their profession. It was also the case that occasionally a company contained an unmarried actress, her presence justified by her exceptional acting talent. Moral considerations also demanded that the costumes worn on stage by actresses had to be seemly. Doublet and hose were forbidden, though masculine costume could be worn from the waist up. As for their behaviour backstage, actresses were allowed dressing-room visits only from their husbands.

The court theatre in Spain really made significant advances with the accession to the throne of Philip III in 1598, for the austerity of his father, Philip II, now gave way to a period of great extravagance. The young queen, in particular, had a great love of theatre, and, because she was unable to attend performances in the *corrales*, she arranged for them to take place in the various royal palaces: in Madrid, Aranjuez, El Pardo, and Valladolid. Initially, these productions were, as they were in the *corrales*, relatively simple affairs, but as time passed they, and the locations in which they were staged, became much more elaborate. With the death of Philip III and the accession to the throne of Philip IV in 1621, this process acquired added momentum. By 1623, the great hall of the Royal Palace in

Madrid had become known as the *salón de comedias*, and
professional companies were performing there at least once
a week, while in the summer of the previous year three
lavish productions had been presented at the palace in
Aranjuez, the Spanish equivalent of Versailles. The
emphasis in these court productions was, as time passed,
increasingly on spectacle, and by 1627 the Italian engineer
and stage-designer, Cosimo (Cosme) Lotti, had been
engaged to create spectacular stage effects. The court
production of Lope de Vega's *The Loveless Forest* in
December of that year involved, for example, perspective
sets, brilliant changes of scene, concealed lighting, and
waves that rose and fell. It was also the first occasion in
Spain when a play had been set entirely to music.

   In 1629 a further development took place when
construction began of a new royal palace in the grounds of
the Buen Retiro on the outskirts of Madrid, a process which
was completed by 1633. Plays were performed there, both
indoors and outdoors, the latter often involving spectacular
effects on the great lake in the park. By 1640, moreover, a
new theatre had been built: the Coliseo del Buen Retiro,
designed by Cosme Lotti. In some ways its structure
paralleled that of the *corrales*, for its shape was rectangular, it
had three tiers of four boxes on either side, and also the area
for women, the *cazuela*, for performances were open to the
public. On the other hand, the stage of the Coliseo was
quite different, for, in contrast to the apron stage of the
corrales, it was distinguished by a proscenium. In other
words, instead of eliminating the gap between the stage-
action and the audience, the proscenium emphasised it,
creating on stage a self-contained world, the illusion of
which was further underlined by perspective scenery. And
this sense of artificiality was further heightened by scene
changes which broke up the action of the play in a way
which was never the case in the continuous, fluid nature of
productions in the *corrales*. In general, the atmosphere
surrounding the performance of plays in the court theatres
was much more formal, as the presence of the monarch
required. Instead of becoming involved in the on-stage

action and resorting to rattles and whistles to express their feelings, the audience became observers and spectators.

An idea of the lavish nature of play productions at court, and of the expense involved in staging them, may be formed from drawings relating to the performance at the Coliseo in 1653 of Calderón's *Andromeda and Perseus*. When the curtain rose initially, it revealed an enormous automaton Atlas, on one knee and bearing on his shoulders a huge globe. The figure then rose and sang. Other scenes included the chamber of Danae, a blazing inferno, Mercury on a cloud which moved around the stage, Perseus rescuing Andromeda from a monster, and a finale in which the gods look down from a stage sky. For productions of this kind, dramatists and acting companies were constantly drawn away from their work in the *corrales* and offered payment and opportunities which they could not obtain there. In the end, therefore, the process had an adverse effect on the public theatres and led to their inevitable decline after a period of vigorous activity that lasted for fifty years.

Just as the public theatres in Spain and England had many things in common, so the development of the court theatres in both countries followed a similar pattern. Cosme Lotti in Spain had his counterpart in England in the architect-designer Inigo Jones, who introduced from Italy the proscenium stage, perspective scenery, indoor lighting, and 'machines', all at vast expense. And, as happened in Spain, this had its effect on the public theatres, transforming play-going from a form of popular entertainment into something much more sophisticated and refined.

'The Duchess of Amalfi's Steward'

Lope's *The Duchess of Amalfi's Steward* is a fine play in its own right, though part of its interest lies, of course, in the fact that it allows for comparison with John Webster's *The Duchess of Malfi*, one of the great plays of the Jacobean period. This said, Lope and Webster were very different in personality and temperament, and also in the vision of the world which their dramatic work presents. *The Duchess of*

Amalfi's Steward, even though it contains much intrigue and ends with the murder of the Duchess, two of her children, and Antonio, her steward and husband, has few of the horrors and the overriding sense of corruption evoked by Webster.

The Duchess of Amalfi's Steward was written between 1599 and 1606, possibly around 1605, when Lope would have been forty-three and an experienced playwright. Webster's *The Duchess of Malfi* was completed in either 1613 or 1614, and was probably performed for the first time either in late 1613 or in early 1614. By this time relations between England and Spain were much closer than they had been two decades earlier, at the time of the Armada, and this, together with certain parallels between the two plays, has led some commentators to suggest that Webster may have known or been told about Lope's play. The absence of any firm evidence to substantiate this possibility makes it rather unlikely.

Lope had a thorough knowledge of Italian and found the material for his play in the twenty-sixth story of Mateo Bandello's *Novelle*, published in four volumes between 1554 and 1573. Entitled 'Il signor Antonio Bologna sposa la duchesse d'Amalfi, e tutti due sono ammazzati' ('Signor Antonio Bologna marries the Duchess of Amalfi and both are murdered'), Bandello's story is as follows: Antonio and the Duchess were married in secret, the ceremony observed only by her ladies-in-waiting. The birth of their first child was successfully concealed, but the birth of the second led to rumours which obliged the Duchess's brothers to place spies in her household. Fearing the worst, Antonio left the Duchess's service to live in Ancona, where, pregnant for the third time, she soon joined him. There she informed her servants of her marriage to Antonio, after which most of them, fearing her brothers' reaction, left her service. Subsequently, the Duchess and Antonio, anticipating banishment from Ancona, escaped to Siena and then attempted to reach Venice. Intercepted en route by armed horsemen, the Duchess persuaded Antonio that her brothers were seeking him, not her, and that he should take their eldest son – by her previous marriage – to Milan. The Duchess and her two other children were then taken to one of her castles, where they were strangled. Antonio, meanwhile, unaware of these events, hoped for a reconciliation with the brothers and a reunion with his wife and children. The brothers were, however, planning his murder, and this was soon effected by a Daniele da Bozolo.

Lope followed the general outline of Bandello's story, emphasising the love between the Duchess and Antonio, their secret marriage, the birth of two children, the couple's escape from Amalfi to Ancona, the Duchess's revelation there of her marriage to Antonio, their attempted escape, the arrest of the Duchess and her two children, and the final murder of all four individuals. On the other hand, Lope modified his source material in significant ways. As the title of his play suggests, Antonio, rather than the Duchess, becomes the main focus of attention, though she too still has a significant role. In addition, the emphasis of Lope's play, doubtless reflecting his own experience, is very much on the theme of love. And, because Antonio's feelings for the Duchess lie at the heart of the action, new characters are introduced who complicate his relationship with her. Ottavio de Medici, for example, is initially unaware of Antonio's love for the Duchess, is himself besotted with her, and persuades Antonio to plead his cause. Again, Urbino, secretary to the Duchess, is in love with Livia, her lady-in-waiting, but is convinced that she and Antonio are having a secret affair, as the result of which Livia has had a child by him. Acts One and Two are largely structured, therefore, around individuals whose desires, jealousies, disappointments, and feelings of betrayal in love both drive the plot forward and create considerable dramatic tension. Furthermore, true to his belief that plays should combine serious and comic elements, Lope offsets the love affairs of the nobles and their associates with the domestic squabbles of peasant characters among whom Antonio and the Duchess live in order to effect their secret marriage, and who are later charged with bringing up their children.

Because the action of Lope's play is much concerned with

these interwoven relationships, the spies mentioned by
Bandello as being introduced into the Duchess's household
by her brothers are absent. Indeed, only one brother, here
called Julio de Aragon, appears on stage, and this only in
the third act, after the Duchess has revealed that she and
Antonio are married and have had two children. The
Duchess's other brother, the Cardinal, is mentioned only by
name. Furthermore, Julio's anger towards the Duchess is
fuelled not by the reports of spies but by Ottavio's sense of
outrage at what he considers to be her betrayal of his
feelings for her. To the very end, then, love and its
associated complications and emotions lie at the heart of *The
Duchess of Amalfi's Steward*.

Lope's ending is rather different from Bandello's. There
the Duchess and her children are strangled and Antonio is
murdered elsewhere. In Lope, Antonio is enticed to Amalfi
in the hope of a reunion with the Duchess and a
reconciliation with her brothers. He and his two children
are then murdered together, and their heads are shown to
the Duchess, who has already been poisoned by her brother,
but who is not yet dead. Quite clearly, Lope based his
ending on another source.

Webster's direct source for *The Duchess of Malfi* was not
Bandello, but the second volume of William Painter's *Palace
of Pleasure*, published in 1567 and itself a translation of
François de Belleforest's *Histoires Tragiques*. This, Belleforest's
version of Bandello, was four times the length of the
original, gave the main characters lengthy speeches and
dialogues, and largely disapproved of the relationship
between the Duchess and Antonio. Belleforest also filled out
the characters, placing much more emphasis on the two
brothers, and presenting Bosola not merely as Antonio's
assassin, as Bandello had done, but as a Judas figure, a
'beast' ruled by covetousness and always available for
murder. Painter's translation remained very close to
Belleforest and provided Webster with all the material he
required.

Webster, nevertheless, made certain important changes in
relation to his source. The Duchess's brothers, Ferdinand

and the Cardinal, are given even more prominence than
was the case in Belleforest/Painter, for in *The Duchess of Malfi*
they appear throughout to oppose, threaten, and torment
their sister. In order to underline the corrupt nature of the
Cardinal, Webster provides him with a mistress, Julia, and,
as a punishment for their sins, he has both brothers die at
the end of the play, a detail nowhere apparent in any of the
sources. Important too in *The Duchess of Malfi* is the even
greater significance given to Bosola, who, though
characterised after Belleforest and Painter, had been in
Bandello only one of a number of spies and agents
employed by the brothers. Webster conflated these roles
into one, introducing Bosola in the very first scene, filling
out his character as a devious and ambitious malcontent,
making him instrumental in the death of the two brothers,
and, as retribution for his evil actions, bringing about his
own death.

As for the presentation of the Duchess and Antonio,
Webster presented the former as beautiful but no paragon of
virtue, for she is reckless in her defiance of her brothers,
and, in her resolve to have Antonio for herself, sexually
driven. In general, Antonio is high-minded and attractive,
but he is given to panicking in moments of crisis and is also
somewhat passive. In the way in which the Duchess and
Antonio are tormented to the end by men as evil as the
brothers and Bosola, Webster depicts a dark and diseased
world even more rotten than Hamlet's Denmark. Bosola is
described as lecherous, covetous, and envious; the brothers
in terms of crooked trees, crows, caterpillars and, above all,
the Devil. Webster, in short, creates a world which is nearer
hell than heaven and in which Bosola's description of the
brothers as having hearts that are 'hollow graves, / Rotten,
and rotting others' is truly appropriate.

Lope's treatment of Antonio and the Duchess is very
different. Antonio is a much more appealing and complex
character than Webster's. The opening soliloquy, in which
he recognises both the folly and the strength of his feelings
for the Duchess, shows him to be an intelligent and
passionate man, torn between his sense of what is right and

his feelings for a beautiful woman. This conflict preoccupies him throughout most of Act One, preventing him from fully revealing his love for the Duchess, but when she reveals her feelings for him, he responds boldly and honestly, accepting the risks that lie ahead. Thereafter, as her husband, Antonio proves himself to be courageous and resourceful in protecting both their secret and their children. And when she later advises him to flee her brothers' vengeance, he at first refuses to do so, arguing that he is obliged to protect his wife and children. In every respect, then, Antonio proves to be a loving husband and father, steadfast in his loyalty to his family. We also learn from the Duchess that he is an excellent administrator, honest, well-mannered, truthful, careful about his appearance, a good horseman, and a skilled musician.

As for the Duchess, her love for Antonio is as genuine and strong as his for her, and there is no suggestion, as there is in Webster, that her passion is sexually driven. On the contrary, Lope's Duchess is a woman of strong feelings and of great integrity, attracted to Antonio not simply by his good looks but also by his qualities. Such is her belief in the genuine nature and goodness of their love, that she is prepared to sacrifice all for it. But, as well as being a faithful and honest lover, the Duchess is also a dedicated mother, concerned for the education of her eldest son by her first marriage, as well as for the upbringing of the two children she has borne Antonio.

Lope's emphasis on the nobility of love is a common theme throughout his work – *Fuente Ovejuna* and *Peribáñez* are other examples – and points to a vision of the world which is ultimately optimistic. Contrary to the impression of reckless, selfish, and irresponsible passion which his many love-affairs might give, Lope was a firm believer in the goodness of love itself and in the sanctity of the family. His relationships with Elena Osorio and Marta de Nevares lasted, after all, for many years, and he cared greatly for the children these affairs produced. In *The Duchess of Amalfi's Steward*, love is therefore presented as generally ennobling, and children, as in the case of the Duchess's eldest son, are seen to be generous and understanding. Indeed, there is no one in Lope's play to match the cruelty and callousness of Webster's Ferdinand, the Cardinal, and Bosola. The one character who can be described as unsympathetic is the Duchess's brother, Julio, and he is clearly disapproved of by those who finally become aware of his treachery towards the Duchess and Antonio.

Just as the Duchess and Antonio are seen to be individuals of dignity and integrity, so their exchanges, both between each other and with others, are distinguished by their intelligence. The language employed by Lope, in accordance with his dramatic theory, has little of the complexity and ornate imagery of later playwrights, but its relative simplicity draws attention even more clearly to the fact that his characters are thinking beings whose conversations, through their wit and ingenuity, constantly hold our attention and, by making us eager to hear more, draw us further into the play. In Act One, for example, both in the exchanges between the Duchess and Antonio, and in Antonio's encounters with Ottavio and Urbino, there is a tension, an element of cut-and-thrust, which is all to do with the quickness of thought of the individuals concerned, but which, at the same time, is the essence and mainspring of drama. It is an area in which Lope was supremely gifted and which makes *The Duchess of Amalfi's Steward* a consistently fine play.

'The Capulets and Montagues'
In 1604 Lope published a list of the 448 plays which he had already written, in which *The Capulets and Montagues* appears at number 395. The date of its composition therefore precedes 1604 but cannot be ascertained precisely. The date of composition of Shakespeare's *Romeo and Juliet* is also unknown, though there seems to be general agreement that it was completed by the second half of 1596. Lope's play may therefore have been written before or after Shakespeare's, but there is no firm evidence, as some critics have suggested, to show that Shakespeare drew, directly or

indirectly, on Lope's version. What parallels and points of contact there are between the two plays may well be due to the fact that such details already existed in the particular sources from which both dramatists extracted their material.

The story of Romeo and Juliet and their warring families had originally appeared, like that of the Duchess of Amalfi and her steward, in Bandello's *Novelle*, where it was entitled 'Romeo e Giuletta'. Lope, as we know, often drew on Bandello for his plots – his dark tragedy, *Punishment Without Revenge*, is yet another example – and there is no reason to think that, given his knowledge of Italian, he did not go directly to Bandello for *The Capulets and Montagues*. In addition, though, Bandello's story appeared in 1559 in a French version by Pierre Boaistuau, published in volume one of François de Belleforest's *Histoires Tragiques*, and this in turn was translated into Spanish and published in Salamanca in 1589 as *Historias Trágicas exemplares, sacadas de las obras del Bandello Verones. Nuevamente traducidas de las que en lengua francesa adornaron Pierres Boaistuau, y Francisco de Belleforest* . . . This would clearly have been available to Lope, and, given his fondness for Bandello's work, it is more than likely that he consulted it.

For his part, Shakespeare used as his direct source Arthur Brooke's long poem, *The Tragical Historye of Romeus and Juliet*, published in 1562, and, to a lesser extent, William Painter's version of the story in the second volume of *Palace of Pleasure*. Painter's story was, in effect, a translation of Boaistuau, Brooke's an expanded version of it in which he made certain additions, expanded existing speeches, and transformed passages of narrative into direct speech. To a certain extent, then, Lope's and Shakespeare's sources had, in Bandello and Boaistuau, a good deal in common, and it is inevitable that there should be certain similarities between the two plays. But there are also very striking and substantial differences which, in the end, are probably less to do with the sources than with the imaginative and artistic predilections of both dramatists.

Lope's Act One corresponds in its general outline to the first two acts of Shakespeare's play, but he also made

significant changes. As was Lope's habit, he plunges the
spectator straight into the action, for it begins with the
masked ball at the home of the Capulets where Roselo
(Shakespeare's Romeo) first sees Julia (Juliet). Shakespeare
places this episode rather later – Act One, Scene Four – and
prefaces it with scenes which emphasise, through the
dialogue and actions of minor characters – the conflict
between the Capulets and the Montagues. This preliminary
material also introduces the hot-headed Tybalt, nephew to
Lady Capulet, who here becomes involved in a skirmish
with Benvolio, a friend of Romeo, and who will later be
killed by Romeo after Tybalt has killed Mercutio in a
sword-fight. Shakespeare's Tybalt is the counterpart of
Lope's Ottavio, who is also hot-headed and is later killed in
a sword-fight with Roselo, but otherwise Lope's presentation
of Ottavio is very different. Firstly, he is attracted to Julia –
Tybalt has no such role – and secondly, Lope develops his
relationship with her at considerable length and along
largely comic lines. During the masked ball at the Capulet
household, for example, Julia's declarations of love are
addressed to Ottavio, who is facing her, but are intended for
Roselo, who is behind her. Furthermore, while she talks to
Ottavio, her hand is extended behind her back and is held
by Roselo. In short, Ottavio is outrageously duped by Julia,
and this is repeated later when, in order to keep him happy,
she speaks to him in the garden between ten o'clock and
midnight, prior to her passionate encounters with Roselo. If,
in Shakespeare's play, the Romeo–Juliet relationship is
highly passionate, Lope introduces a comic element which is
quite distinctive.

    His treatment of the events which lead to Roselo's
banishment from Verona is also substantially different from
Shakespeare's. Shakespeare begins Act Three with an
encounter in the street between Tybalt, Mercutio, and
Benvolio, which then leads to the sword-fights in which
Tybalt kills Mercutio, then Romeo kills Tybalt. In Lope's
play, early on in Act Two, there is also a sword-fight in
which Roselo kills Ottavio, but this stems from a dispute in
church between the Capulets and Montagues over a private

family chair which the Capulets accuse the Montagues of
abusing. In Shakespeare there is no church and no chair,
and if there is a similarity in both plays in relation to
Roselo's/Romeo's reluctance to fight Ottavio/Tybalt, there
is also a difference in his escape from the scene, for Lope has
him take refuge in a tower, Shakespeare in Friar Lawrence's
cell. Thereafter, both dramatists have him banished from
Verona, and both have an attempt by Julia's/Juliet's father
to arrange her marriage to Paris. In Lope's play, though,
Roselo's life is saved by Paris as Roselo travels into exile: an
incident which has no parallel in Shakespeare.

Lope's Act Three and Shakespeare's Act Four coincide in
that they focus on the sleeping-draught consumed by
Julia/Juliet and her burial in the family tomb in the belief
that she is dead. But subsequently the two plays diverge
significantly. In Act Five of *Romeo and Juliet*, Romeo is
informed of Juliet's death, fails to receive the letter from
Friar Lawrence which tells him that she is merely asleep,
and purchases a poison in order to end his own life. He then
visits Juliet's tomb, is confronted by Paris, kills him, and
drinks the poison. When Juliet awakens and learns of
Romeo's death, she commits suicide.

In contrast to Shakespeare's tragic ending, Lope's is much
more comic, entirely optimistic, and quite unexpected.
Having been informed that Julia is merely asleep, Roselo
visits her tomb in order to rescue her. She, surrounded by
corpses, wonders if she is dead or alive, and, hearing voices
approach as Roselo and his servant draw near, thinks they
might be ghosts. This comic episode is also heightened by
the fears and antics of the servant. Subsequently, Julia
encounters her father, has him believe that she is a spirit
from the other world, informs him that, prior to her death,
she had married Roselo, and makes him promise that he
will never harm the young man. The promise secured, Julia
then reveals that she is alive, her father is overjoyed and
accepts the marriage, and the play ends optimistically with
the reconciliation of the Capulets and Montagues. This
ending, as well as being highly amusing, would have been,
with its emphasis on an apparition, both dramatic and

entertaining for a Golden Age audience.

The essential difference between Lope's and Shakespeare's plays is summed up by the fact that *Romeo and Juliet* is entitled a 'tragedy' and *The Capulets and Montagues* a 'tragicomedy'. There are, of course, comic elements in the former, notably in the characterisation of the garrulous Nurse, but the predominant tone of the play is serious, increasingly so as the action unfolds and the emphasis is placed more and more on the way in which the lovers are caught up in the events which lead to their deaths. Lope's 'tragicomedy' is, as the word suggests, a mixture of serious and comic elements which in the end become, not a tragedy, but the triumph of love. Throughout the course of the play, obstacles are placed in the way of Roselo's and Julia's love for each other, and these, as in the case of Ottavio's desire for her, are often presented comically. This is not, though, to suggest that Roselo's and Julia's relationship is portrayed as light-hearted, but rather that they are called upon to emerge victorious from a series of situations which are sometimes comic and absurd, and sometimes threatening. While Shakespeare's play is largely even in its overall trajectory, Lope's is much more of a roller-coaster in which he amuses, delights, and surprises a demanding audience by often changing direction. In this respect, it is a very different play from *The Duchess of Amalfi's Steward*, which Lope described as a 'tragedy', and in which there are therefore very few comic elements. Even so, *The Capulets and Montagues* is yet another example of Lope's constant fascination with the theme of love. In some ways, the opposition of the Capulets to Romeo is reminiscent of that of Isabel de Urbina's parents to Lope's desire to marry her, and in that case too the lovers overcame such opposition.

As far as characterisation is concerned, there is no doubt that Shakespeare's play is superior to Lope's. In some cases, Shakespeare's characters are admittedly little more than the stereotypes he inherited from Brooke. Tybalt and Paris are typical examples, the former a hot-head, the latter a rich and honourable gallant. Neither are the Capulet and

Montague parents much more than stereotypes concerned about their children's future. But elsewhere Shakespeare created some rounded and memorable characters, such as the talkative, opportunist, obsequious and sensual Nurse, and Friar Lawrence too, whose role as moral commentator is so at odds with his rash behaviour. Most attention, though, was clearly devoted to Romeo and Juliet, both of whom come alive on the page, as well as the stage. From a self-effacing, undemonstrative girl of barely fourteen years of age, Juliet matures through her love of Romeo into a much more committed and thoughtful character, fully aware of the dangers attending her relationship with him but wholly given to it. Romeo himself, though some six years her senior, is in general less mature, but he is equally committed, both in life and in death.

Lope was, in general, more concerned with providing the theatre audiences of his day with a plot which would hold their attention, which meant in turn that characterisation was often subordinated to a fast-moving and complicated action. But this is not to say that Lope was incapable of creating memorable characters, as plays such as *The Duchess of Amalfi's Steward* and *Punishment Without Revenge* suggest. In *The Capulets and Montagues*, Roselo and Julia are less fully drawn than Romeo and Juliet, but this does not mean that they are unconvincing as dramatic characters. In Act One, Julia reveals herself to be astute and spirited in handling the advances of Ottavio, while at the same time declaring her feelings for Roselo; and he, in responding to her, proves to be equally sharp. Similarly, at the end of the play, Julia shows remarkable ingenuity in pretending to be a spirit from the other world and in obliging her father to accept Roselo as her husband. As for Roselo, he is courageous, steadfast, often sensible, and, in the garden scene with Julia in Act Two, very much the ardent lover. Shakespeare's more detailed characterisation is due in part to the fact that he devotes more space to the lovers, but Lope's presentation of them is also more than assured.

The language of *The Capulets and Montagues* is, like that of *The Duchess of Amalfi's Steward*, largely straightforward and direct, though sufficiently varied in relation to whether given situations are serious or comic. The presence of Marín, Roselo's servant, during the scene in the tomb, is guaranteed to involve exchanges of a comic nature. Ottavio's impulsive attack on Roselo in Act Two is expressed in urgent, quick-moving terms. And the scenes between Roselo and Julia are effective in their simple yet intense expression. Thus Roselo to Julia in the garden scene in Act Two:

> I know you'll weep when I am gone,
> But dry your tears now before
> Your sobs are overheard and I
> Am seen . . . (ll.397–400)

Shakespeare's language, when Romeo sees Juliet at her window in Act Two, Scene Two, is more poetic:

> But soft, what light through yonder window breaks?
> It is the east, and Juliet is the sun.
> Arise, fair sun, and kill the envious moon,
> Who is already sick and pale with grief . . . (ll.2–5)

But this in no way invalidates the quality of Lope's language, which, if less weighty and poetic, can be more incisive and to-the-point than Shakespeare's.

'Cleopatra'
Rojas Zorrilla's *Cleopatra* – the literal English translation of the Spanish title, 'Cleopatra's Asps', would be unintentionally comic – was first performed in 1640 and published in the 'Segunda parte', the second volume, of his plays in 1645. Shakespeare's *Antony and Cleopatra* was written much earlier, either towards the end of 1606 or in the early part of 1607, though it did not appear in print until 1623. The subject was, of course, a popular one in both Spain and England. The Spanish dramatist, Diego López de Castro, had written *Marco Antonio y Cleopatra* in 1582 – there is nothing to suggest that Rojas knew it – and in England the

Countess of Pembroke's *The Tragedy of Antonie* and Samuel
Daniel's *The Tragedy of Cleopatra* were completed in 1590 and
1594 respectively. As well as this, the principal figures in the
story – Octavius Caesar, Mark Antony, Cleopatra – were of
great interest to sixteenth- and seventeenth-century writers,
not merely on account of the love story of Antony and
Cleopatra, but also on account of the political issues which
that story involved and the relevance they had to
contemporary England and Spain.

The story of Antony and Cleopatra had originally been
described at length in Plutarch's *Lives*, a semi-fictional rather
than a factual treatment of history written between AD 110
and 115. Rojas Zorrilla may well have read Plutarch, but it
is also possible that he was familiar with a Spanish source:
Alonso de Castillo Solórzano's *Historia de Marco Antonio y
Cleopatra, última reina de Egipto*, published in Zaragoza in
1639, one year prior to the first performance of Rojas' play.
As for Shakespeare, his direct source was a translation by
Sir Thomas North, published in 1579, of a French version
of Plutarch's *Lives* by Jacques Aymot. Rojas' and
Shakespeare's treatments of the story are, however, very
different, the Spanish dramatist departing from his source
material much more than his English counterpart.

Act One of Rojas' play begins with the return to Rome of
Antony and Octavian (Shakespeare's Octavius), Antony
having defeated the king of Persia, Octavian having been
defeated by Cleopatra, who has also defeated Lepidus, the
third member of the Roman triumvirate. But if these
opening scenes appear to emphasise war, their real focus is
the theme of love and the bond of friendship between the
three men, and between Antony and Octavian in particular.
Lepidus is in love with Octavian's sister, Irene – Octavia in
Shakespeare – but his love is unrequited, for she is in love
with Antony. Octavian, though vanquished by Cleopatra, is
still dazzled by the memory of her beauty, and promises
Antony that, if he can overcome Cleopatra, he can keep her
lands provided that he hands over Cleopatra. Meanwhile,
he arranges Irene's marriage to Antony.

The second half of Act One introduces Cleopatra, who,

far from being a temptress, is portrayed as a beautiful and chaste woman, for she has decreed that in her kingdom all sexual relationships outside marriage shall be punished with death. Her views are reflected in her judgements on several of her subjects, one of whom, condemned to death, predicts that Cleopatra will herself fall victim to love and will be poisoned by asps. The act ends with the arrival in Egypt of Antony and reveals their immediate attraction to each other.

The arrangement and emphasis of Rojas' material here is quite different from Shakespeare's. In Act One of *Antony and Cleopatra*, Antony is already with Cleopatra in Alexandria, while in Rome Octavius decries Antony's absence and way of life, demanding that he return in order to assist him and Lepidus to counter the threat posed by Pompey. In Shakespeare's Act Two Antony returns to Rome, he and Octavius patch up their differences prior to confronting Pompey, and it is decided that Antony shall marry Octavius' sister, Octavia. Cleopatra in Alexandria is enraged by reports of the marriage, while Pompey, threatening Rome, accepts the triumvirate's offer that he become ruler of Sicily and Sardinia.

Unlike Shakespeare, then, Rojas begins his version of the story well before Antony and Cleopatra meet, and he emphasises too the close bonds of friendship between Antony, Octavian, and Lepidus, none of which is present in Shakespeare's play. Furthermore, although Shakespeare begins his play with the love-affair of Antony and Cleopatra, much of the first two acts focuses on politics and war, in particular on the threat represented by Pompey. In *Cleopatra* the political theme is barely mentioned, and Rojas' emphasis is almost entirely on the love theme embodied in the interwoven relationships of Lepidus, Irene, Antony, Cleopatra, and Octavian. Cleopatra is also presented in a way which is very different from Shakespeare. Shakespeare's wily, teasing, and very jealous queen is portrayed by Rojas as initially chaste and dismissive of love, an aspect of her character which serves, of course, to emphasise her surrender to it when she meets Antony at the end of Act One.

The love theme continues to dominate Rojas' second act.
It begins with the arrival in Egypt of Octavian, Lepidus, and
Irene, who soon discover that Antony, captivated by
Cleopatra's beauty, has decided to stay with her rather than
return to Rome – the situation presented by Shakespeare at
the beginning of Act One. From this point on, Rojas' play
becomes a revenge tragedy in which love betrayed becomes
the mainspring of the action. Octavian, having asked
Antony to deliver Cleopatra to him, feels betrayed, as does
Irene, promised to Antony in marriage, while Lepidus, in
love with Irene, resents Antony for ending his hopes of her.
All three therefore plan revenge on both Antony and
Cleopatra, who realises that her subjects will never allow her
to marry Antony, and so they plan to escape to Asia. The
act ends with Octavian and Irene attacking Alexandria by
land, while Lepidus launches a naval attack on Cleopatra's
ships.

In *Antony and Cleopatra* Octavius' hostility towards Antony is
motivated by politics, not love, and is exacerbated by the fact
that Antony, having taken Octavia with him to Athens, then
tires of her and sends her back to Rome. By this time
Lepidus has been dismissed by Octavius from the
triumvirate, and Pompey is dead, all of which leaves Antony
and Octavius as the two principal adversaries. Consequently,
much of Shakespeare's Act Three is concerned with
Octavius' ultimately futile attempt to turn Cleopatra against
Antony after he has defeated him in a sea battle. It is a very
different scenario from that of Rojas' Act Two.

Rojas' third and final act resembles Shakespeare's Acts
Four and Five only in that it presents the defeat and the
deaths of Antony and Cleopatra, for the detail is otherwise
entirely different. Act Four of Shakespeare's play sees
Antony defeat Octavius' troops outside Alexandria, but he is
then defeated in a second confrontation. Convinced that
Cleopatra has betrayed him, Antony is so enraged, that she
flees and takes refuge in a tomb. He is then mistakenly
informed of her death and commits suicide. In Act Five,
Octavius commands that Cleopatra be brought before him,
but in the meantime she poisons herself with an asp. In

Rojas' final act, Octavian, Irene and Lepidus defeat and
capture Antony and Cleopatra. Octavian and Irene decide
to separate them, he taking charge of Cleopatra in the hope
of winning her love, Irene keeping Antony prisoner in the
hope of rekindling his feelings for her. At the same time,
Lepidus, still in love with Irene and resenting her proposed
marriage to Antony, arranges his and Cleopatra's escape,
thereby removing him from Irene's attentions. As they
attempt to flee, Cleopatra seeks to create a diversion by
making her pursuers think that she has thrown herself into
the sea. Antony, convinced that she is dead, kills himself,
and Cleopatra, finding his body on the shore, presses the
asp to her breast.

If, as has often been said, Shakespeare drew heavily on
Plutarch's account of Antony's life, albeit via Sir Thomas
North, Rojas clearly did not. Shakespeare undoubtedly
reshaped his source material, shortening it and elaborating
the roles of the two lovers, but his debt to Plutarch was still
substantial. Rojas, on the other hand, proceeded very
differently, departing from the historical account as he saw
fit, and producing what is on the whole a new version of the
story in which all the main characters are part of the love
theme. While Shakespeare focused on love in relation to
Antony and Cleopatra, Rojas placed them at the centre of a
number of entwined relationships which push the political
aspect of the story into the background, though this is not to
say that the two main characters are given less importance
than in Shakespeare. It is rather the case that the rest of the
material and the other characters are substantially changed
in order to fit around the protagonists. As for
characterisation, Antony and Cleopatra are in general
impressively drawn, both initially dismissing love but later
overwhelmed by it to the extent that, rather than survive
alone, they welcome death. In addition, Rojas' concentration
on the love theme means that *Cleopatra* is, if anything, more
tightly structured than its English counterpart, which at
times seems somewhat rambling. Not for nothing has Rojas
been compared with Calderón, whose plays, in plot and
structure, have an almost mathematical precision.

As far as language is concerned, Rojas belonged to a cultural period, the Baroque, in which the language of poetry – and therefore of plays written in verse – had become much more ornate and image-based than had been the case in Lope's time. Indeed, he learned much from Calderón, whose language was distinguished by its pattern and symmetry, its stylisation, and its brilliant imagery. The following description of Antony's fleet as it approaches Alexandria is typical of Rojas' style, in which, as in Calderón, ships parting the waves are described as leaping fish or birds skimming the water, and brilliantly coloured objects are compared with bright jewels:

> See there.
> A fleet of ships. I'd say two hundred at
> The very least. They seem like gulls
> That skim the waves, or fish that pierce
> The air. And at their head a ship
> Which, more a bird of pine than feathers, turns
> The bright blue water into snow-white foam.
> Its stern displays red flags that gleam
> Like rubies in the sun. Its prow
> Adorned with ivory, its oars
> With silver, its rudder gold, it rivals
> The sun in all its splendour. (Act One, ll. 746–57)

Much of the play's imagery – allusions to the sun, light, flowers, plants, and precious stones – forms a network of allusions which suggest the magnificence of Cleopatra's Alexandria, her dazzling beauty, and the sensual nature of her love-affair with Antony. It is fair to say that, in its language, there are many passages in *Cleopatra* which invite comparison with Shakespeare.

Given that Rojas was very much a court dramatist, it is more than possible that *Cleopatra* was first performed at one of the court theatres. The Coliseo del Buen Retiro was, after all, completed in 1640, when his Romeo and Juliet play, *The Factions in Verona*, was performed there, though there is no solid evidence to indicate that the same was true of *Cleopatra*. But it is clearly true to say that a well-known story about

Roman generals, empire, and an exotic queen, would have
appealed greatly to Spanish royalty and the court as a
whole. And one can well imagine the staging of certain
scenes in the play in a theatre whose resources were much
greater than those of the *corrales*. Such is the scene at the end
of Act Two, when, as Alexandria burns and smoke covers
the sea, Cleopatra and Antony call out to and vainly search
for each other, their voices carried away on the wind. And
equally impressive is the final scene in which the lovers
escape independently in the darkness, Cleopatra's clothing
is seen floating in the sea, Antony kills himself, and
Cleopatra, having discovered his body on the shore,
commits suicide. These are brilliantly dramatic scenes which
cry out for the kind of facilities afforded by the court
theatres. However, this is not to say that *Cleopatra* could
not have been performed in a simplified staging in the
corrales.

The translation
Golden Age plays consist, on average, of some three
thousand lines, each of their three acts of a thousand lines or
so. For the most part, if not entirely, lines are of eight
syllables, and the dramatists of the period, from Lope de
Vega onwards, employed a variety of stanza forms which
ranged from three to ten lines and involved complex rhyme
schemes. It would be foolish of any translator to attempt to
reproduce the stanza forms and rhyme schemes of the
Spanish original, for this would merely result in a highly
stilted and probably unspeakable translation. On the other
hand, the retention of the octosyllabic line is desirable,
for it creates, when spoken, the kind of pace which Lope
and his disciples thought essential. In these translations,
therefore, I have largely, if not entirely, opted for lines of
eight syllables, but, in the interests of flow and relative
naturalness in the language, I have rejected stanza forms
and rhyme schemes.

   In general, the aim of these translations is to provide
those interested in theatre with versions of Golden Age plays

whose subjects have their counterpart in Elizabethan and
Jacobean drama, and to offer acting companies texts which
are speakable. My hope is that they capture the spirit of
Lope de Vega and Rojas Zorrilla.

The Duchess of Amalfi's Steward

A tragedy

Lope de Vega

Characters

Antonio, *the steward*
The Duchess
Ottavio de Medici, *a suitor*
Urbino, *secretary to the Duchess*
Julio de Aragon, *brother to the Duchess*
Livia, *servant to the Duchess*
Celso, *an old servant to the Duchess*
Furio
Dinarco } *servants to the Duchess*
Filelfo
Ruperto
Duke of Amalfi, *son of the Duchess*
Alejandro, *son of the Duchess*
Leonora, *daughter of the Duchess*
Fabricio, *servant to Ottavio*
Lucindo, *servant to Antonio*
Fenicio, *servant to Julio*
Bernardo, *friend of Antonio*
Doristo
Melampo } *peasants*
Arsindo
Bartola

Act One

Antonio
I am just an ordinary man,
And yet I dare aspire to the sun.
For this I shall be punished, made to see
The earth grow dark. My eyes, like Icarus,
Have gazed on beauty far beyond my reach.
Like him I'll fall, my hopes extinguished in
A sea of tears.
Pity the common man who tries
To catch the wind but catches fire!
These eyes have been too free, have looked
Too often on the Duchess. A servant in
Her house, I've stared at heaven when I should not.
But she's encouraged me in this, not in
So many words but in the sweetness of
Her smile, and only because of that do I
Now dare to love what is impossible.
Pity the common man who tries
To catch the wind but catches fire!
Trained to be attendant to the Court,
I served her uncle, Frederick, King   20
Of Naples; followed him to France
When he was overthrown, and then
Returned, weary of such a life.
The Duchess, already widowed, and her son
Still young, requested that I serve
Her as I'd served her uncle. But little did
I dream, although I had her confidence,
That I would feel this love, this mad desire.
Pity the common man who tries
To catch the wind but catches fire!

Enter **Ottavio de Medici**, *his servants, and* **Fabricio**.

Ottavio
So is Antonio here?

Fabricio

He is, my lord.

Antonio

As ever at your service, sir.

Ottavio

Then you reciprocate my love for you.
Today, my friend, my fears give way
To hope. And hope provides the solid ground
On which I plan to build my happiness.

Antonio (*aside*)

A marriage to the Duchess, that's his plan!

Ottavio (*to his attendants*)

Leave us! We need to speak alone.

Antonio

What would you have me do, my lord?

Ottavio

Antonio, as you know, I am   40
The nephew of the Duke of Florence . . .

Antonio

And, as I also know, an honest man . . .

Ottavio

I shall inherit his estate quite soon,
And now Amalfi's dead and leaves
A widow and a son so young . . .

Antonio (*aside*)

My fears are justified!

Ottavio

                                        . . . I think
The Duchess shall become my wife.

Antonio

In that case, sir, I must be frank.
The Duchess is, of course, still young
And beautiful. But if the management

Of her affairs, now in my hands,
Should pass to someone else, her son
Shall cease to be her ward, and, more
Than that, she loses her estate.
In short, she will be poor, and you'll
Inherit nothing.

Ottavio

Quite possibly,
But seeing her will be enough. I shall enjoy
The riches of her beauty.

Antonio

Love makes
You speak like this, my lord. The fact
Is any obstacle, like heavy rain   60
In hot July, merely increases the heat.
But let that heat-wave pass and in
A month or so you will be calm
Again, regretting what then seems
A temporary madness. Besides,
Imagine the effects of poverty:
Living in some obscure town
Where no one ever visits you.
You'll find the flame of love
Soon fades. And then regret will put
An end to any love you might have felt.
Believe me, sir, to place such faith
In passion is to fly a kite.

Ottavio

Antonio, I haven't called you for advice,
Not when my mind's made up. In any case,
You are too young to know much better than
Myself. But since you are her steward you
Must know her mind. I thought it best
To tell you of my plans. But I
Admit, it never crossed my mind   80
How much you have to lose. I understand
Your opposition, misguided as it is.

Antonio
You do me a disservice, sir.
Self-interest plays no part in this,
Rather my devotion to the house
Of Aragon. It's true that I'm
Not rich, but not so poor that I
Depend on her estate and wealth.

Ottavio
Then I am even more surprised
That you oppose my love for her.
What can you gain from it?

Antonio
                              Gain, my lord?
Please say no more!

Ottavio
                  Why be concerned
If we are forced to live in poverty?

Antonio
So be it! Marry her! Marry ten
Times over if you wish.

Ottavio
                    But can't
You see my love is genuine?

Antonio
Indeed I do! What else would drive
A man to such a foolish act?

Ottavio
Is that what you intend to tell her?

Antonio
My duty is to do what you   100
Command.

Ottavio
              Then speak to her on my
Behalf.

Antonio

You may rely on me.

Ottavio
Persuade her . . .

Antonio

You have my word.
If I have any influence,
I'll plead your cause.

Ottavio

If you succeed,
You'll have a suitable reward,
A chain of pure gold! Farewell.

Exit **Ottavio**.

Antonio
It seems I have no choice. If only these tears
Would form a sea where I could drown!
And yet this is a plank to save
My life, to put an end to this
Mad passion! For once she's married, love
Will be in vain, and so, the cause
Removed, must die! But even so,
I need to know her thoughts on marriage.
My hope, though small, is not extinguished!

Exit **Antonio**. *Enter the* **Duchess of Amalfi** *in widow's weeds;*
Livia, *her maid; and* **Celso**, *an old man.*

Duchess
Where is my son?

Celso

At his lesson, my lady.

Duchess
Which one?

Celso

Grammar, I believe.

He's learned to write and so must also learn
The rules that govern language.

Duchess

Good.   120
A prince should have a good command
Of Latin.

Celso

He recites so well
He'll soon have mastered it. The boy
Has one of the sharpest minds in Italy.

Duchess

In that he follows his father.
But tell his tutor he must also learn
The use of arms.

Celso

Indeed! A boy
Who's master of both pen and sword!
If I could only shuffle off the weight
Of all my years, I'd teach him all
The skills of swordsmanship.

Duchess

So were you known for that?

Celso

I had
No equal in the whole of Italy.
But now my sword's become this cursed stick!
I fenced with the best, but finally
I find myself fenced in by age.

Duchess

Speak with the tutor. See he carries out
My wishes.

Celso

I'll do it now, my lady.

Exit **Celso**.

Duchess

Oh, Livia, how I suffer for this love!

Livia

I hate to see you long for someone far   140
Beneath your rank. Besides, if you
Are weak, how shall I contend with love?
To be a widow and still so young is so
Unfortunate.

Duchess

            You really think
That mere weakness makes me risk
Offending God and damaging
My reputation?

Livia

          To send for him
Is madness. What do you intend to say?

Duchess

I think you know.

Livia

           And you must know
You risk your life. The marriage is unseemly.

Duchess

I think you rather fancy him yourself.

Livia

Oh, no, my lady! I swear to heaven.
I've never fancied him at all!

Duchess

Livia, you know I've always trusted you,
Shared all my thoughts.

Livia

           And so you always can,
Madam.

Duchess

     My secrets have been yours.
I've told you what I barely dared
To tell myself. And if I said you might
Have fancied my Antonio, that
Was just because I do believe   160
His qualities are such he'd melt
The heart of any woman. He's so
Well-spoken, so good-looking.
He writes so perfectly, and never fails
To carry through the tasks he sets
Himself. You cannot but admire him!
And then his manners, his honesty,
His sense of truth, his style, his dress.
The way he rides, his grace, his gift for music!

Livia

Oh, madam, such ecstatic praise
Amazes me almost as much as he
Amazes you! But if your cruel fate
Obliges you to place your wealth
And power in your steward's hands,
At least take care you keep the matter secret.

Duchess

Our marriage shall put an end to all
These fears. It shall be done in secret,
And by the time the secret is revealed,
I'll be his wife.

Livia

     Let's hope it's not his death.
Oh, madam, I'm so afraid. I'll not   180
Encourage you nor try to change
Your mind. But there are many who
Desire you, and many of higher rank
Than your Antonio.

Duchess

     I know

That marriage to a servant goes
Against my rank, and most would say
My honour. But marriage is to show
Respect for honour, as well as fear
Of God. If only He and you know of
My plans, my secret's safe.

Livia

Let's hope it is, my lady.

Enter **Antonio**.

Antonio

My hopes, still cold, fly up – a moth
Towards the flame, towards the sun
Of those bright eyes. The man who dares
To look on them must share the pride
Of Lucifer before his fall from grace.
I go where I shall burn, yet everything
I see persuades me to be bold and gives
Me strength. As legend says, the satyr saw
A flame, grasped it, and when it burned,   200
Released it, crying out in pain.
But who would grasp the flame of love
Like this, and when it burned, not grasp
It even more? . . . Ah, is the Duchess here?

Duchess

Antonio!

Antonio

              I wish to speak to you alone.

Duchess

Of course. Livia, wait outside.

Antonio

Sweet heavens! Her beauty blinds me!

Livia

Consider who you are. Be sensible.

Duchess
Enough of this advice. Leave me!

Exit **Livia**.

Why so surprised?

Antonio
      At simply being here.

Duchess
What? Have you never been before?

Antonio
Of course. But never quite like this.
It makes me nervous.

Duchess
      Nervous of me,
Antonio? You think me sharp, quick-tempered?

Antonio (*aside*)
Rather, her beauty unsettles me.

Duchess
I am your mistress, true, which may
Cause some concern. But then, of course,
A woman's gentle nature overcomes
A man's timidity. So do you think
Me overbearing, stern, unduly proud?   220

Antonio
You know what makes me so afraid.
When someone draws a curtain to reveal
An angel, the sight of such divinity
Will make him tremble. While grim and terrible sights
Inspire fear, beauty too can be the cause
Of it.

Duchess
    But you have seen me often enough.
Is my beauty any greater than it was?

Antonio

At other times there were others present.
But when I find myself alone
And in the presence of a beauty that
Is more than mortal, my thoughts begin
To fly beyond the realms of common sense.
But even so, our thoughts are free. There is
No blame attached. They cannot cause offence.

Duchess

Antonio, must I feel offended if,
As a man, you think of me as a woman?

Antonio

I suppose not. But you understand my fear.
You are, my lady, noble and
Discerning.

Duchess

      Oh, come along, Antonio!
What's all this 'noble and most discerning'? Talk   240
To me familiarly. I am your mistress, yes,
But do I sit upon my title as though
It were a throne? As for discerning, some
Would say I am, but rarely can
A person be completely so.
To tell the truth, I've often made
Mistakes. I mean, how often can
One trust a woman's judgement? But as for you,
You've governed my estates most wisely. That's why
I've summoned you. In future you and I
Must set aside our differences of rank
And act much more as equals. Understood?

Antonio

I don't know what to say. It feels
So strange. My duty is to kneel
At your feet.

Duchess

      Antonio, I insist you speak

To me on equal terms. Away
With courtesies.

Antonio

                    I am afraid that if
You favour me like this, my thoughts
Might easily become too bold and make
Me say what I should not. There is,   260
My lady, something you should know.

Duchess (*aside*)
He understands. I see by his
Expression and his tone of voice.
I have revealed my meaning clearly.
That ought to be enough to make
Him speak more openly. But still he will
Not speak. When love commands, a man
Must be a fool to hesitate so much.

Antonio
The truth is, madam, I've been asked
To speak to you. Ottavio de
Medici sent for me . . .

Duchess (*aside*)
                    What does he mean?

Antonio
He has requested me to speak on his
Behalf . . .

Duchess (*aside*)
            Why this? Perhaps he doesn't love me.
I know he feels for me and knows
My mind as if I'd spelled it out
For him. But even so, until
I'm sure of his love for me, I can't
Declare my feelings openly.

Antonio
If honour allows my petition, madam, this
Is what I have to say. Ottavio is   280

A man of many qualities.
He's sensible, reliable, and brave.
But, more than that, he says he worships you,
Wants you to be his wife, and, as
A dowry, asks for nothing more
Than your person.

Duchess (*aside*)
                    He says this is
Ottavio's suit. It seems more like
His own. (*To* **Antonio**.) Antonio, every man
Should have the right to state his love
To whom he wants.

Antonio
                    And so Ottavio states
His love for you, and being of equal social rank,
Would have you for his wife.

Duchess
                    A man
Who's not of equal rank could equally
Declare his love if it were genuine.
True love can never be wrong.

Antonio
                         Quite true. But what
If love is just desire, nothing more,
And only seeks to satisfy itself?

Duchess
That would depend upon the judge
To whom the man in question put
His case. Assume the woman he loves   300
Is also the judge. The verdict would
Be hers. Antonio, you confuse me!

Antonio
I don't know why, my lady.

Duchess
                    Speak

To me on equal terms, not merely as
My steward.

Antonio

   I cannot.

Duchess

      Why ever not?

Antonio

I am afraid to do so.

Duchess

      Afraid of what?

Antonio

Of what might happen if I ceased to be
Afraid.

Duchess

   I see. My frankness disturbs you.

Antonio

I have to know what I must tell
Ottavio.

Duchess

    In that case, pay attention.
Imagine you are setting out
Upon a journey, by land or sea.
You fully intend to go alone,
But then, quite unexpectedly,
Two travellers appear and ask
If they may keep you company
Along the way. For one of them
You feel a natural attraction.
His looks and conversation give
You pleasure. The other you detest.   320
To be with him would fill you with
Despair and even horror. So which,
If you must choose, goes with you on
The journey? The one you like, or the one

You hate?

Antonio
The answer's clear enough.

Duchess
So tell me. Which one would you choose?

Antonio
The one I liked the most.

Duchess
Which is
Exactly what I choose to do. Marriage is,
In my opinion, such a journey. I have
To choose between two men, who could
Not be more different from each other.
Ottavio is the one I hate.

Antonio
Then who is it you like?

Duchess
You mean
I haven't made it clear enough?
Your wits must be completely dulled.

Antonio
Not dulled, my lady. Blinded by
Humility.

Duchess
Perhaps the mention of
My marrying a second time
Is difficult. A note shall tell
More clearly who it is I love.   340
Wait here.

Exit the **Duchess**.

Antonio
Oh, why so cowardly? Heaven blast
My foolish hope! To have the prize

Within my grasp and then draw back! My suffering
Is well deserved! The man who loves,
Is loved, and dares not speak, must lose!
Why, opportunity is like
A woman with a single lock
Of hair. When she comes close, you have
To grasp it quickly or she's gone.
What hope is left for me? What debt
Is there for me to claim when I
Have cancelled this? The man who hesitates
Is lost, and lost for good. Her note
Will tell me this. Oh, I deserve this fate!
Love grants no second chance, not when
It calls and I then fail to answer it.

Enter **Livia** *with a note.*

Livia
A note, Antonio, from my mistress.

Antonio
I think she is upset by my
Suggestion of a second marriage.   360
For that I'm sorry, Livia.

Livia
                She says
She's named in this the man she loves.

Antonio
I had her happiness in mind,
No more. The house of Medici is
Most suited to her rank.

Enter **Urbino**, *secretary to the* **Duchess**.

Urbino
                The girl's
In love with him! She's given him
A note. Livia, wait!

Livia

What is it now?

Urbino

I see my doubts are justified. You gave
Antonio a note.

Livia

Did I?

Urbino

As well as that,
The tenderest of looks!

Livia

To the note
I admit, to the looks I do not.
In any case, Urbino, men see what they want
To see. The note was just an order for
Material for a gown. Good day!

Exit **Livia**.

Antonio

I am cursed in this from the very start!
He must have seen her give me the note.

Urbino

Antonio!

Antonio

Ah, good secretary!

Urbino

A secretary who, as good friends do,
Knows how to keep a secret. I think
That Livia loves you.

Antonio

Why should you   380
Think that?

Urbino

Because she yields to you.

Antonio
I don't know what you mean.

Urbino
                                        I saw
Her yield a note to you, a love-note I
Suspect.

Antonio
              Then I confess. I find
Her quite attractive.

Urbino
                            You know that I've
Been courting her!

Antonio
                        Ah, yes, of course.
I take your point. All right, she's yours.
I yield her to a better man.

Urbino
Then I accept. But only if, since we
Are friends, you do not suffer from
This act of generosity. And I
Must know as well that nothing else
Has passed between you.

Antonio
                              Just this note,
My friend.

Urbino
              No other notes?

Antonio
                              Urbino, this
Is all she's given me.

Urbino
                  I'd like
To read it if I may . . . and if
You value our friendship.

Antonio
                    You don't
Believe me! My word should be enough!
Why so suspicious? I shan't go near her.

Urbino
Then tear it up, Antonio, still   400
Unopened. That's all I ask.

Antonio
                    I'll tell
You what, my friend. I'll tear her from
My mind. As for the note, I cannot tear
It up. To do so would be disrespectful to
The sender. And against my principles.

Urbino
I thought you were my friend, Antonio.
Because of that I asked this favour.
But now that you've refused, I cannot be
Your friend. You have offended me
Much more than I can say.

Antonio
                    No, wait,
Urbino.

Urbino
        What is it?

Antonio
                    If we aren't friends,
And I am not obliged to you,
I'm free to fancy Livia even more.

Urbino
Then do it. But I promise you,
One day I'll do the same and wound
You in the place that's closest to
Your heart.

Antonio

          Urbino, listen. Hear
Me out. I'll not reply to you
In kind. I always say that when
One friend is in a rage, the other must   420
Be right. But even so, I'll prove
That I'm both gentleman and friend.
Instead of contention, we shall share
The content of the note. I'll break
The seal. I'll read it first, then you
Shall see it too.

Antonio *rips off the part of the paper which contains his name.*

          It's very brief.
Here, read it.

Urbino

         You tore some off.

Antonio

                Oh, just
Seven letters.

Urbino

       So what is this?

Antonio

            The rest
Of it.

Urbino

     But it's completely blank.

Antonio

There could be meaning in its lack
Of words. A secret code one has
To solve. Perhaps there was nothing more
To say.

Urbino

     Antonio, stop tormenting me!

What's written on your piece of paper?

Antonio

I've told you, just seven letters.

Urbino

Is

That all?

Antonio

It is.

Urbino

Then if you are
My friend, tell me the first.

Antonio

I think
The last two letters first. This is . . .

Urbino

An 'o'.

Antonio

And this . . .

Urbino

An 'i'. I need the other five.

Antonio

What, tell you five? Am I some kind   440
Of clock? I've given you two. Be satisfied!

Urbino

Give me the rest, you'll be my friend
For ever.

Antonio

Friends should share things equally,
So seven divided gives you three. The half
That's left we'll split.

Urbino

Damn you! I need

Them all!

Antonio
          All right, no need to get upset.
Two more. An 'n' and an 'o'. There,
You have the last four letters.

Urbino
                              But are
They in the right order?

Antonio
                    I'm not
Quite sure. You'll have to work it out.

Urbino
    I need the other three!

Antonio
                    That would
Be far too easy. (*Aside.*) The message says
'Antonio'. In short, she chooses me
To share her journey with. Urbino has just
Four letters, nothing there to use
Against me. The note contains my name,
No more, but quite enough to make
Her meaning clear. The risk is that
Her brothers should find out and punish me
For such presumption. But still, what better way   460
To risk one's life? (*Aloud.*) Farewell, Urbino.

Urbino
    God be with you.

Exit **Antonio**.

He thinks I cannot understand it.
'O, i, n, o'. It's meaningless.
But Livia and the Duchess are
Both Spanish and Antonio knows
The language. I think I see it now.
'O, i, n, o' becomes 'Hoy no',

Which means, translated, 'Not today'.
She means they cannot meet today.
But what about the other letters,
The three he's kept? Let's see. Reverse
The 'n' and 'i' and what we have
Is 'onio'. So if the other three are 'a, n, t',
The seven would make 'Antonio'. I'm sure
That's right. It makes good sense. But what's
It mean, the name alone? It makes no sense,
Unless this is some cunning trick to drive
Me mad. I shall throw water on this fire
And raise more smoke: the water from   480
My eyes, the fire from my heart, the smoke
From all my smouldering frustration!
I swear they'll pay for this. I'll watch
Antonio's every move. He has
Betrayed our friendship. The Duchess has
To know that such disloyalty
Could also be disloyalty to her.
I'll sow mistrust in her and have
Him banished. Ah, here she comes. The chance
Presents itself.

Enter the **Duchess**.

Duchess

My soul's on fire, now I've revealed
My feelings to Antonio. I fear
This passion will betray me, bring
About my death. But if I marry and
Do not offend my honour, such a love
As this is worth the sacrifice.
Ah, here's Urbino. What news, secretary?

Urbino

No news, madam. Have you replied?

Duchess

I've given it much thought. It's not
An easy matter. My son is still   500

So young.

Urbino

Your brother is concerned
For your future.

Duchess

I know he is.

Urbino

As well as for the boy's.

Duchess

I'll give
My answer soon.

Urbino

I think he wastes
His time in trying to persuade you.
You seem opposed to any marriage.

Duchess

It doesn't interest me. I never think
Of it. Besides, my son is far
Too young to know if he would want
A Medici for a father. As for
Myself, I'll not be pressed on anything
So personal.

Urbino

I understand. But still,
I'm sure you'd like to know about
Another marriage soon to be arranged
In your household?

Duchess

What marriage?

Urbino

I'm sorry it upsets you.

Duchess

You mean

A woman in my house intends
To marry without my knowledge?

Urbino
To be quite fair, both individuals
Are honourable people. Besides,   520
They marry for love.

Duchess
                I'm sure they do.
Who are they?

Urbino
           Antonio and Livia.

Duchess
They told you this?

Urbino
               They did. I've seen
Them too. But understand, I tell
You this in confidence.

Duchess
               Your secret is
Quite safe with me. (*Aside.*) Oh, how this tests
My patience! (*Aloud.*) What exactly did
You see?

Urbino
          Livia gave Antonio a note.

Duchess
And when was that?

Urbino
           A moment ago.

Duchess
Thank you, Urbino. Leave me now.

Urbino
My lady, don't be angry. I thought
It right to do my duty to my office.

Duchess

I know what's happened. Antonio's not
To blame.

Urbino

The way you offer him
Protection . . .

Duchess

How dare you be so impudent!
Just go! And when you bring reports
Like this, be sure there's better proof.

Urbino

I told you what I saw, my lady.
I thought such secrecy an insult to this house.
And such affairs are ended much   540
More easily if stopped in time.
Why, I'd report my father if
He acted like Antonio.

Enter **Antonio**.

Antonio

Your carriage has arrived, my lady.

Duchess

Thank you. I thought some country air
Might do me good, but perhaps I'll change
My mind. Secretary!

Urbino

Madam.

Duchess

I have
No wish to make my brothers angry.
Inform them I'm not feeling well,
The reason for my failure to reply
So far. I must find some solution to
Their plans for me. As for yourself,
Do not speak badly of someone who speaks well

Of you – better than you deserve!

Urbino

I'll write the letter.

Duchess

Antonio! Forget
This marriage!

Exit **Urbino**.

Antonio

My lady, I don't know what
You mean.

Duchess

The matter of the note . . .
You have mismanaged it. Urbino saw you.

Antonio

Livia was to blame for that.

Duchess

You should
Have been more prudent. You failed   560
To respect my honour and position.

Antonio (*aside*)

How fickle women are! Just as
The sunflower follows the movement of
The sun, so female whims dictate when they
Feel love or hate! (*Aloud.*) Madam, I think
I have misread the situation. You wrote
My name, but now I see you have
Committed more to paper than to me.
The note was like a heart, my name
Another heart at its very centre.
I thought it a sign of love, and I thought too
That the hand which formed the letters
Was a hand offered in love to me.
I see how wrong I was, the joy I felt
Misplaced, my name as empty of love

As the blank paper it was written on.
'Antonio', the letters inky black,
Seems more the inscription on my grave.
The paper's whiteness is my pale fortune,
The blackness of the ink my folly!   580

Duchess
Enough! You held my reputation in
Your hands! You carelessly abused it!

Antonio
My sole offence was holding back,
Not daring to reveal my feelings,
Believing myself unworthy of your love.
But now, before another day is done,
You'll be Ottavio's, and then you'll see
Me scorch and burn for having missed
The opportunity. I'll go away
So you will never hear my name.
And then, because I'll never see
Those eyes again, my life shall end,
As surely as Absalom's, hanged by
His hair.

Duchess
            Antonio, wait!

Antonio
                        Why must I wait?

Duchess
Be patient, please!

Antonio
                There is no place
For patience!

Duchess
            I know you love me, but
You have to treat me differently,
Ignore my rank. You act with diffidence,
Expecting me to use the honeyed words

That more become a man. Be bold!   600
Speak out! Tell me you are dying of love!
In matters of love men always rule,
Declare themselves, while women are
More modest in their words. But we
Have feelings too, and what we most
Dislike are men who are imprisoned by
Their fears and doubts, and so avoid
An open declaration of their feelings.

Antonio

The truth is, madam, fools are much
Too bold, and much too bold because
They are such fools. But if you are
Displeased by my humility;
If I seem guilty of a lack
Of boldness, lacking the courage to speak
When I already knew your love
Was mine, I'll be the opposite! I'll take
Your hand, I'll dare to hold you close, I'll make
Your mouth a flower to the eagerness
Of my desire.

Duchess

                    Antonio, no!

Antonio

But why? You said . . .

Duchess

                    You go too far!   620

Antonio

Then I shall be your servant as
Before. Forgive my foolishness!

Duchess

Oh, back once more to where we were,
The mill-wheel round and round again!
But love must speak. There is no force
Can silence it. Antonio, I love you, yes,

But understand I cannot love
You openly, as you suggest.
If you are seen embracing me,
I am dishonoured. Our love must be
In secret. And, more than that, if we
Are not to cause offence to God,
We must be married. You know that if
My brothers learn of this, my life
And yours will be lost. We have
No friends in them. The pity is
That love is often ruined by
Its cause, by lovers who, longing for
Each other, give themselves away.
Should we produce a child there'll be   640
No choice. I shall declare you are
My husband. But in the meantime we
Shall consummate our love in such
A way that no one else shall know of it.

Antonio

What you suggest is right, as well
As honourable. But I have reasons too
To keep our love a secret. If I enjoy
The beauty of your heaven, why would
I want to share that knowledge with
Another person? I'll guard it jealously
And be content with my good fortune.
Today you've shaped my life anew,
As surely as heaven once gave me breath.
You give me dignity. Can I believe
That I'm your husband?

Duchess

                              As from today
I shall be yours. All differences
Of rank and station are eclipsed
By our destiny. But still, we need
To find a way to manage this,
So we can marry secretly.   660

Antonio

> I think there is a way to keep
> Our secret and avoid the scandal that
> You fear. We'll go to my estate.
> We can disguise ourselves and live
> Among the ordinary people,
> The peasants who work the fields,
> The shepherds who guard the flocks.
> When we are known to them and to
> The local priest, he'll marry us.
> My happiness will be complete!
> I cannot wait a moment longer!

Duchess

> The plan is excellent. We'll leave
> Tonight, dressed in peasant clothes. When we
> Are married there, we shall be happily
> And blamelessly united in
> The honest bond of marriage.

Antonio

> So how will you explain your absence?

Duchess

> Livia shall inform the household I
> Am sick, confined to bed.

Antonio

>   Ah, yes,
> A most effective remedy!   680
> And when the night is at its darkest and
> The world's asleep, we'll take two horses.

Duchess

> Go, get them ready now!

Antonio

>   And clothes!
> I'll see to it.

Duchess

>   The water's wide

But love demands we reach the safety of
The shore. God be with you, Antonio!
Be careful, do not trust the servants!

Antonio
Love shall be my only guiding light.

Duchess
Oh, how I love you, Antonio!

Antonio
May fortune love me half as much!

Duchess
Death is nothing if I die for you.

Antonio
No, death will then be life. God keep you!

Duchess
And protect you!

Exit **Antonio** *and the* **Duchess**. *Enter* **Melampo** *and*
Arsindo, *two old peasants, and* **Doristo**, *a youth.*

Melampo
Arsindo, out of my way! I'm going
To kill this good-for-nothing boy.

Arsindo
Come on, Melampo, show him how fond
Of him you are.

Doristo
                    Oh, this is great!
He only wants to kill me!

Melampo
                        God smite
You to the ground and blast you to
Eternity.

Doristo
                Please, granddad, keep   700
Your cool! What's the point of this?

Melampo

You show me no respect, that's what!

Doristo

So how should I respect you, tell me.

Melampo

By taking my advice, of course.

Arsindo

I'd like to know what this is all
About.

Doristo

      Me wanting to get married.
He don't approve of it.

Melampo

            He wants
To be a cockerel while he's still
Inside the shell. His mother married at
The age of forty, when she was good and ready.

Doristo

If she heard that, she'd say it was
A lie.

Melampo

      Which means that you are calling me
A liar!

Doristo

      It's not that, granddad. It's just
That women marry when they're fourteen.
I reckon she was fifteen, 'cos I'm
Fifteen, and mother's thirty now. So all
That stuff about her being forty when
She married can't be true, 'cos that
Would make her fifty-five, and that
She wouldn't like at all, not when
She's only thirty. And if she married at
Fifteen, and I'm fifteen, it follows that . . .

720

Melampo
For God's sake, boy . . .

Doristo
                              Well, all I want
To say is that you cannot make
Her older than she is. The passing of
The years are just like sins – they show
Upon a woman's face. But she's
No marks on hers because she's not
As old as you pretend. In any case,
It's not the old days now, granddad. Times
Have changed and people like a bit of fun.
In your day they may have married at thirty
Or forty. But now we like to speed
Things up a bit. Why baby girls,
Still at their mother's breast, look up
And say: 'I need a man.' So parents try
And keep up with things, but all
To no avail, for daughters nowadays
Have independent minds and choose
What man they like, not have him chosen.   740
Anyway, granddad, look at me.
I've whiskers growing on my face.
I want to marry. I've got my reasons.

Melampo
What reasons?

Doristo
          I'm in love.

Melampo
                    Have you
No sense of shame?

Doristo
          Not really, no.

Arsindo
Melampo, it can't be bad to marry for love.

Doristo

Believe me, Arsindo, I have to get married
Today. Why heaven demands it, even if
Granddad objects to it.

Arsindo

                    Melampo, see
Some sense! The boy's made up his mind.

Melampo

What could be worse?

Arsindo

                    Why's that?

Melampo

                              His house
Will be a mess. But, more than that, a babe
In arms will never make his bride
Content. You speak to him.

Arsindo

                              Ah, yes,
Of course. My boy, your granddad thinks
You're far too young. He's not against
You getting married in the future.
But at your present age he feels
Your failure will bring shame upon
Us all.

Doristo

                    I don't know what you mean.   760
What failure?

Arsindo

                    You not being man
Enough to satisfy a wife.

Doristo

                              Is that
What he's afraid of?

Arsindo

                              Exactly that!

Doristo

I'll tell you now, then, seeing she's
Your daughter. The house might be a mess,
It's true, but as for being capable,
I'm capable all right. She's pregnant.

Arsindo

She's what?

Doristo

I'm sorry. I couldn't help it.

Melampo

I don't believe a word of it.
She's made it up, to make you marry her.

Doristo

Oh, come on, granddad! If you were in
Her state, they'd come from Rome to marvel at
The spectacle.

Arsindo

Look, both of you!
This isn't funny. Bartola is my one
And only daughter.

Melampo

So is this true?

Doristo

It could be, yes. One night I met
Her on the road to town. I got her in
The bushes, just a bit of fun it was,
And now she says she's carrying a child,
And everyone's gone mad!

Melampo

I'll kill her!   780

Doristo

All this is unbelievable. Why, first
Of all, they say I'm far too young
To marry. And now I'm not allowed

Because I've proved I'm not too young.
I'm being punished all because
I did wrong but did it right.

Arsindo
There's only one thing matters. We must
See honour satisfied.

Melampo
                    I wash
My hands of it. Go fetch the priest!

Enter **Antonio** *and the* **Duchess** *in peasant dress.*

Arsindo
I'm on my way.

Exit **Arsindo**.

Antonio
We'll ask the peasants. It's safe
Enough. Is this the way to the village?

Melampo
Our friend is headed there. He'll show you.

Doristo
He's going to fetch the priest.

Antonio
                         Ah, yes?
A happy event, I trust.

Melampo
                  At least
It's not a death!

Antonio
              Congratulations!
How long before he gets here?

Melampo
                      About
An hour.

Antonio

> I have a plan.

Duchess

> Tell me!

Antonio

We'll intercept the priest along
The way. I shall pretend I'm dying from   800
A mortal wound, and since I fear for
My soul because we are not married, beg
Him that he'll marry us at once.
He will ignore the banns and we
Shall be husband and wife.

Duchess

> A pretty plan!

Antonio

Let's go and wait for him.

Exit **Antonio** *and the* **Duchess**.

Doristo

So who will be my best man?

Melampo

> Best fetch
Your uncle, together with your best suit.

Doristo

I don't know if he's there. I think
The Duchess's steward sent for him yesterday.
I'll go and see.

Melampo

> Let's hope he is.
He can bring your aunt.

Doristo (*aside*)

I'm sorry, my darling Bartola,
For saying you are when you aren't!

Act Two

Enter **Ottavio de Medici**, **Urbino** *the secretary, servants.*

Ottavio
You did inform her there are letters from
Her brother?

Urbino
                    I did indeed, but she
Ignores such things. Her illness is
Her one concern.

Ottavio
                    I'm sorry to hear
She isn't well. They say that absence makes
The heart grow fonder. How true that is!
Two years I've been in Rome, and in
That time my love for her has grown
Much deeper. Now that I'm back and my
Affairs are finally resolved,
I've asked her brother, Julio, if
He'll give permission for my marriage to
The Duchess. He says he is agreeable
If she also agrees to it. But since
He knows she has no wish to marry,
He's written in support of my petition,
Hoping to change her mind. I'd like
To deliver his letters myself.

Urbino
She's been like this for two months.
No one's allowed to visit her.   20

Ottavio
Urbino, speak to her on my
Behalf. She needs to bear in mind
My love for her and my position.
If you speak up for me, you will
Persuade her. If not, my love will prove
An even stronger argument.

But is this illness genuine,
Or simply a device to keep
Me at a distance? Two months, you say,
She's been confined to bed. It makes
Me think my coming back has made
Her sick. Tell me what you think.
Is she so ill because of me?
There's nothing worse than an unwanted suitor.

Urbino

I do believe her illness is
Quite genuine. In fact, I'm quite
Surprised you didn't know of it.
You can't expect to see her today,
But I'll make sure she gets the letters.
Should she improve, she may agree   40
To speak with you tomorrow.

Ottavio

I'm not convinced. Two years I've been
Away, her health was good. And this
As soon as I return!

Urbino

                    Not so, Ottavio.
About a year ago she had
Another illness, the cause, I think,
A melancholic humour.

Ottavio

                    Perhaps
Because she lost a husband at
So young an age. So are you in
The habit of advising her?

Urbino

No, not as much as formerly.
I think I may well leave her service.
To be quite frank, she rarely asks
For my opinion. Antonio is
Her chief adviser, her right-hand man

In everything. I have effectively
Been made redundant.

Ottavio

He is a good
Man, is he not?

Urbino

Undoubtedly.

Ottavio

Much praised for service to the kings
Of Naples.

Urbino

I do not doubt he merits his   60
Success. But even so, he does me wrong
In courting someone I myself
Have hopes of marrying.

Ottavio

That must
Be Livia.

Urbino

It is, but she does not
Alleviate my torment.

Enter **Antonio**.

Antonio

My lord Ottavio. The Duchess, as
You know, has been unwell. She feels
She cannot speak with you today
Because her illness does not grant
Her peace of mind. But she assures you
You'll be informed as soon as she
Improves. She'll see you then.

Ottavio

I understand.
I thought perhaps her illness was
Assumed, a good excuse in order not

To see me now. But since it seems
Quite genuine, convey to her
My hopes for her recovery.
It will not do to have a lady greet
A suitor in her bed. Tell her I
Shall send her gifts meanwhile.   80

Antonio
I shall, my lord.

Ottavio
                    Farewell, then, gentlemen.

Exit **Ottavio**.

Antonio
God protect you, Urbino.

Urbino
                    Not so
Much me, Antonio. Better He
Protect our friendship. Now we are
Alone, I'll tell you what I think
Of your behaviour.

Antonio
                    No doubt
This has to do with love and its
Ability to lead us all astray.
Just think, Urbino. The clouds we see
Above assume strange shapes. We give
Them names: 'serpent', 'ship', or 'cows',
Or 'men'. Well, as I see it, those
In love create such clouds as well,
And they are called 'suspicion' or
'Betrayal' and the like, which in
The end dissolve because they have
No substance. In short, Urbino, ignore
Imagination and its tricks. I have
Done nothing to offend you.

Urbino

Oh, no?
I think you are the crocodile   100
Which weeps false tears while devouring
Its prey. You see, I sought permission from
The Duchess for Livia's hand, but was
Informed that you were soon to marry her.
If that's the truth, Antonio, you are
No friend of mine, rather the hypocrite
Whose honeyed words conceal his true
Intentions.

Antonio

Urbino, I am not
To blame. I did not ask for Livia's hand.
I think the Duchess may have seen
It as a suitable reward for my
Good work. But she's mistaken. I'm no
In love with Livia. She'd be a burden.
I promise you, I will not marry her.

Urbino

If you refuse, she'll feel offended!

Antonio

But why, if I've not asked for her?
Besides, if she believes she's being forced
To marry me, she might complain
Herself.

Urbino

So do you think my hopes
Are still alive?

Antonio

I'd say, alive   120
And kicking.

Urbino

Then I'll approach the Duchess once
Again.

Antonio

> Don't forget, I am your friend, Urbino.

Exit **Urbino**.

> This situation is so full of danger!
> Two years have passed since our secret marriage.
> I've never known such happiness!
> What man would not be envious
> Of my good fortune? We have a son
> Who, since his birth, has lived away
> From here, raised by others in the mountains.
> And now the Duchess, pretending to be ill,
> Has had a girl, so beautiful
> She is a tiny miracle. The two
> Of them are incomparable,
> The one the sun, the other the moon,
> Both lighting up the world with their
> Good looks and innocence. But now it's dark,
> I must conceal my little girl,
> My tiny moon, and carry her
> Away to safety. The night shall have
> No cause to fear her light will drive   140
> Away its shadows. She'll be concealed
> Beneath my cloak until I reach
> The hills where she will share her brother's life.

Exit **Antonio**. *Enter* **Urbino**.

Urbino

> The Duchess's plans to marry Livia to
> Antonio drive me mad. He says
> She doesn't interest him, but even so
> I must be sure. I need to know
> The truth, to test if what he says
> Is genuine or false. He swears
> It's true, but any lover knows
> That passion can betray the best
> Of friends. This is where, in better times,
> I met with Livia, this the meeting-place

Where we declared our love. I think
That if Antonio really plans
To marry her, his words to me
At odds with his desires, this place
Is where they'll meet, as we once did.
His explanation may be just
A trick, pretending that he's forced   160
To marry by the Duchess. If this
Is true, I shall prevent it. If false,
I'll demonstrate a sword can cut
As deeply as a lying tongue!
What's this? Someone's opened the secret door.
It leads to a staircase, and that
In turn to the Duchess's chamber.
What can this mean?

Enter **Livia** *with a baby in her arms.*

Livia

     Antonio!

Urbino

It's Livia's voice. She calls Antonio!
So this is what he meant by 'forced to marry'!
What more is there to say to justify
My fears? Oh, God! You see how I'm
Deceived!

Livia

     Antonio!

Urbino

      I'll play along
With her, pretend that I'm Antonio.
Why not if she deceives me? (*Aloud.*) Here!
I'm here!

Livia

     Take the child. I can't stay. Goodbye.

Exit **Livia** *after giving the child to* **Urbino**.

Urbino

This is a dream, a figment of imagination!
She said a child. If so, a child
Born into hell, matching my own fate!
Oh, this is worse than I expected!   180
I thought to find Antonio wooing her
With tender words. Instead, a child,
Its tiny cry the proof of how he lied to me.
Men often learn their fate through words,
But here I hold the very fruit
Of their sweaty labours, delivered first
To her and now to me. The living proof
Of their guilt, the evidence
Whose eyes and hands and feet condemn
Their lust and treachery. They say
Love and suspicion father jealousy,
But now, in me, they both combine
To make me feel the very pain
Of childbirth, this child the offspring of
Their secret love and my suspicion.
Throughout the ages men have longed
To see this creature we call jealousy.
Some say it takes the form of spectacles
Whereby the smallest thing is magnified.
Some say it is a prism made   200
To trick a lover's eye, others envy,
Or trust that once existed but is lost,
A monster bred from fear and hearsay.
But now I say that anyone
Who thinks that jealousy is all
These things, should come and see
Its living form embodied in
This child. But someone's coming. No doubt
Antonio.

Enter **Antonio**.

Antonio

I hope I'm not too late. At every turn

Ottavio plagues me, urges me
To plead his cause for marriage to
The Duchess . . .There's someone here! Perhaps
Ottavio's followed me again. This is
Most strange. No one ever comes here
At night. What's he doing? You, sir!
What do you want? The Duchess is
Confined to bed. The presence of
A stranger here offends the honour of
The house. I saw you from the balcony.   220
I'm her steward and protector. Be off with you!

Urbino

You call yourself her steward? I call
You traitor. You have betrayed me, Antonio!

Antonio

Urbino! What are you doing here?

Urbino

Discovering how false you are!

Antonio

But I've done nothing to deserve
This accusation.

Urbino

          My sword should speak
On my behalf and punish you
For what you are . . . a treacherous liar!
But see how full my hands already are
Of your blood! If only it could be
A sword, it would avenge me all
The better! Livia called as I stood here,
Obviously mistaking me
For you, and gave me this. Antonio, she
Gives birth to your child while you
Pretend to me that she is being forced
On you. Oh, what a stratagem!
You pleasure her, as she does you,
And yet you claim to be aggrieved   240

Because the Duchess wishes to
Arrange your marriage. Affairs like this
Are commonly known as 'palace fruit',
Which signifies how sweet they taste,
But this is no such dish, nor is the man
Who's helped himself an honest guest!
Here, your child! Never say that we
Were two against you. This child is part
Of you. Holding it offends me, but it
Is innocent, you alone the object of
My vengeance. You speak of honouring
This house, yet this is how you honour it!
Perhaps I should have kept the child and shown
The Duchess proof of your infamy.
So small a creature, feather-light,
But proof enough of your levity.
Make no mistake, I shall inform
The Duchess of all this . . . of how
Her faithful steward is the cause
Of my distress and her dishonour!   260

Exit **Urbino**.

Antonio

My God! What can I do? For two
Whole years our love has been a secret,
But one mistake in just one day may well
Destroy it all. Yet fortune could
Have smiled on me, for what has happened here
Has missed the mark. Urbino's love
For Livia blinds him to the truth,
And jealousy distorts his view
Of things to my advantage. I am
Indebted to his doubts. The storm
To which he is exposed is my safe haven.
Anxiety has blinded him,
For when he holds the Duchess's honour in
His hands, he thinks it's Livia's, she
The one who is to blame. And since

The Duchess knows the truth, it's not
Important that he speaks to her.
I shan't become the object of
Her rage, nor will his longing for
Revenge on me be satisfied.   280
But now I must ensure the safety of
My child. If I am seen or they
Discover where she's gone, my fate
Is sealed. She is a tiny book
Where all my secrets are concealed,
And which must not be read by anyone.
She is the ledger where I've entered my
Accounts. It must be hidden from
The public gaze, or else the Duchess and
Myself could find ourselves, because
Of our dealings, exposed to bankruptcy.
Come, little one. I'll take you to
Your brother and the peasants in
Their mountain home. They are such good
And honest people. You'll be safe
With them. Heaven shall protect you for
Much greater things; and anything
That heaven protects will surely
Be safe from harm.

Exit **Antonio**. *Enter* **Doristo**, **Bartola**, *and peasants.*

Doristo

I have to go to town, Bartola. Stop   300
These tears!

Bartola

                        It shows what sort of man
You are.

Doristo

                Don't be so silly! You are
My wife. I took an oath to spend
My life with you, till death do us part,
For better or worse. And this is worse!

Bartola
You said you'd love me too, and only me.

Doristo
Did I say that?

Bartola
                    You see? You can't remember.

Doristo
In any case, it's you I love. Everyone knows.

Bartola
You go away, abandon me, and then
I start imagining.

Doristo
                    You've got no cause.

Bartola
Doristo, I can't help myself.

Doristo
It's jealousy, my sweet, the green-
Eyed monster. But that's for city-folk,
Not us.

Bartola
            Not true! 'Cos where there's love,
There's jealousy, as surely as day
Turns into night. Do you know what love
Would be if there weren't jealousy?
A clock without its wheels, a hook
Without its onions, a cupboard with
No crockery. Or else, a house without   320
A roof, a garden with no gardener,
A mortar with no pestle, a stove
Without a fire, a font without
Its water, a tart without her rouge,
A pan without its oil, a distaff with
No wool, fried bread without some bacon,
An invalid without an illness,

A drum without a drummer, an ass
Without a pack, a cabbage with
No leaves, a farm without a farmhouse,
A man and wife without a family!
That's love without its jealousy.
Is that enough for you?

Doristo

              Oh, very good,
Bartola! I can't believe how bright
You are. Have you been studying?
The priest's books, I reckon, when you
Were in his study.

Bartola

             Wrong, Doristo!
Love's been my teacher all along.
You'll never know how hard its lessons are.

Doristo

I bet the priest's been teaching you   340
Some things!

Bartola

           The workings of the heart
Are studied in the school of suffering.

Doristo

My God! That's deep!

Bartola

            And all of us
Are pupils in the school of love.

Doristo

Yes, yes, I understand. But even so,
I need my freedom. A woman shouldn't keep
Her husband in the house. You see,
A man who sees his wife the whole
Day long begins to think she's not
As pretty as he thought she was.
She seems much less a woman than

A chair, or the wooden board on which
She kneads her bread, or the rack in which
She keeps her ladles. And so it's best
A man is free to go outside, and see
His wife afresh when he returns.
Besides, just think of all those things
That, when a husband sees his missus all
The time, get on his nerves. The way
She does her hair before the mirror,   360
And all those clips and pins, and jars
And creams. All right, we don't mind when
She's done and looks agreeable,
But we don't want to see what leads to it.
A woman's looks are like a pie: best served
When done, but spare us all the stuff
Goes into it. Anyway, as far
As I can see, women are all
The same: in great demand before
They marry; very demanding afterwards.
Look, people coming!

Bartola
                              It's just one person.
He's come on horseback.

Enter **Antonio**.

Antonio
                              I rode as fast
As possible, but daybreak's still
Outstripped me. I doubt that I was seen.
Ah, two peasants! Good morning, both!
Which is Bartola's farmhouse?

Bartola
                              He must
Be lost.

Doristo
          He seems to know you.

Bartola
I think it's the master.

Doristo
                    It is.

Bartola
Welcome, my lord!

Antonio
                    Doristo! Bartola!
How is my little boy?

Doristo
                    He's almost grown   380
A beard.

Bartola
            He's well. In no time at all
He'll be in charge of the threshing.

Antonio
And your baby?

Bartola
                    We buried him
Six days ago.

Doristo
                    Either my misfortune or
Our destiny. They said he ought
To enter the Church, one day he'd gain
By it. Well now the Church has gained by him.
He's theirs till the Day of Judgement.

Antonio
I'm so sorry! I've been so fortunate!

Bartola
If someone needs a wet nurse, send
The baby here. I weaned your boy
Just eighteen months ago, and see
Him now – an elephant!

Antonio

> The fact is,
> Bartola, there's someone here who needs
> You for exactly that. My little girl,
> The boy's sister. The sun above
> Needs company, so here she is,
> A shining star.

Bartola

> Here, let me take her!
> Oh, bless the child! Who would have thought
> Good fortune would have smiled on us?   400

Doristo

> Go on, give her a lucky charm!

Bartola

> More like a thousand! God protect her!
> Look at her laughing! She wants to talk
> To me.

Antonio

> Finding you here bodes well,
> I think.

Bartola

> By my grandfather, I swear
> She wants my milk. Look how her eyes
> Are shining bright! My little love,
> My empress, my sweet little duchess!

Antonio

> Excellent!

Doristo

> Just listen to this wife of mine!
> Just two days old, she thinks she's talking,
> And asking for her milk. This kind
> Of nonsense-talk turns women's brains,
> You know. The baby gives a little cough,
> They swear it's just said 'Dadda'.

Antonio
    Let's go! I want to see my son.
    You'll need this money to take care
    Of them.

Doristo
              Where's your horse?

Antonio
                          Tethered to
    The tree. He's safe enough.

Doristo
                    We can see
    Him from the house. The herders can keep
    An eye on him.

Bartola
               Lily and carnation all   420
    In one! It's just as if she's mine,
    Doristo. A living child is such
    A comfort! Oh, by the way, you can go now,
    Wherever you want.

Doristo
               You can't be serious!

Bartola
    Oh, but I can! This little one
    Is all I want.

Doristo
            So you don't love me!

Bartola
    It's not that I don't love you, no.
    I love this little one more, that's all.

Doristo
    Oh, well, if that's the case, I'll find
    A little girl that I can love –
    Sixteen or thereabouts!

Exit **Antonio**, **Bartola** *and* **Doristo**. *Enter the* **Duchess** *and*
Urbino.

Duchess
If the author of this secret is
Ottavio, you'd best not tell me.

Urbino
He's not, my lady. I think you mock
Him, as well as those who speak to you of marriage.

Duchess
So what's the nature of this secret?

Urbino
I have to say that, joyful as
We are that you are well again,
It grieves me to upset you with
This news.

Duchess
                    You think it will upset me?   440

Urbino
Unless, of course, you wish to see
It in a different light. A wise
Old man depicted understanding with
A pair of scales: on one scale, chance:
Wrecked ships and mighty fortunes lost,
Great reputations overturned,
Vast empires won, great victories
And triumphs. On the other scale,
A feather . . .

Duchess
                    Urbino, you are most
Annoying!

Urbino
                    Why will you never listen?

Duchess
Go away!

Urbino
                    All women are the same
When they hold power. The day
Will come when you'll regret dismissing me.

Duchess
    All right, speak up!

Urbino
                    My one concern
    Is your well-being.

Duchess
                    Perhaps. So what
    Is this that's so important?

Urbino
                    Last night
    I was mistaken for Antonio. Livia called
    Me on the terrace and handed me
    The proof of her wrongdoing.

Duchess
                    What proof?

Urbino
    A new-born baby wrapped in   460
    A blanket.

Duchess
            Really? Whose child was it?

Urbino
    Why, hers of course. And I believe
    That both of them have sinned in your house,
    So damaging its reputation.

Duchess
    You say a baby?

Urbino
                Indeed. I thought
    Of bringing it to your chamber.

Duchess
Perhaps you dreamt it all.

Urbino
                    Maybe.
That must be why, still dreaming, I drowned
It in a ditch.

Duchess
                You what?

Urbino
                    If it was all
A dream, killing the child would hardly matter.

Duchess
If it were true, my name would be
Of less importance than compassion for
The child.

Urbino
                It isn't true. The only truth
Is Livia's infamy. Antonio came
To get the child.

Duchess
                Where is it now?

Urbino
I handed it to him.

Duchess
                    You acted properly.
One has to act according to
God's will. He sacrificed His son
For such a child's salvation. As for
Myself, my honour is betrayed.   480
Antonio had my confidence,
Yet seemingly does this. Bring Livia here!

Urbino
My lady, should the members of
Your household get to know of this,

All Italy in turn will know of it.
The consequence will be that some
Malicious individuals will speak
So badly of this house that your name
And honour will be lost.

Duchess
                        Then what
Do you advise? Do you think I ought
To call my brothers?

Urbino
                        To remedy
An ill as yet unknown to others,
I do believe that secrecy is best.

Duchess
I'll have him put to death.

Urbino
                        By far
The safest course of action.

Duchess
                        No, no,
I think not. That would merely cause
Suspicion. Besides, Antonio is
A gentleman, a man of standing.
Far better that they marry.

Urbino
                        Do that
And some will think you must have known   500
Of their infamy; that you condone
Such immorality.

Duchess
                        Then you suggest
What I should do.

Urbino
                        Get rid of him,
Once and for all.

Duchess
>   Well said! But Livia shan't
> Know why. First we shall dismiss
> The steward, then I'll take revenge
> On both of them. I value your advice,
> Urbino. I haven't done so in the past,
> But now you shall control my house,
> Chief steward in Antonio's place,
> My confidant. Have the servants come,
> Antonio too!

Urbino
>   This is by far the best
> Solution. As you well know, discretion is
> The better part of valour.

Exit **Urbino**.

Duchess
> Oh, my Antonio! What could be worse
> Than this? Just minutes late
> Arriving to collect our child
> Has led to this! But even so, no
> One knows the truth, so why complain?
> It could be worse by far. Our secret might   520
> Have been revealed the day my son
> Was born, but we were careful then
> And so avoided it. But now the pleasure of
> My daughter's birth has given way
> To fear and risks my honour. Perhaps
> It's no surprise that she should cast
> A shadow on her father's life,
> When, as we know, a woman is
> The origin of man's misfortune.

Enter **Furio**, **Filelfo**, **Dinarco**, **Ruperto**, **Urbino**, *and*
Celso.

Urbino
> I've brought Ruperto, Furio,
> Filelfo and Dinarco.

Furio
>   Your wish
> Is our command, my lady.

Duchess
>   It seems
> That I embark on my dishonour. Why has
> Antonio not arrived?

Filelfo
>   They say
> He's been away and only just returned.

Enter **Antonio**.

Antonio
> My lady, you wish to speak to me?

Duchess
> Antonio, I am upset. I may
> Seem calm but, as you know, appearance
> Can easily deceive.

Antonio
>   So why
> Are all these servants here?   540

Duchess
> Because there will be changes in
> My household and they must be informed.
> Furio, you served the Duke, God rest
> His soul, most loyally. For that
> You are retained. This is, of course,
> A woman's house, more difficult
> To manage than before, but you
> Have served me well.

Furio
>   My lady, may
> I speak? We are your trusted servants.
> Could it not be that some mistake,
> Quite trivial in itself, has been

Exaggerated? I find all this
Most strange.

Filelfo

Perhaps some person in
Your confidence invents these lies, which in
The end will be no more than windmills.

Duchess

Believe me, the matter rests on solid ground.
But you are wise and loyal too.
I find no fault with you. You'll serve
Me still.

Filelfo

I am indebted.

Dinarco

My lady,
I feel ashamed to have suspicion cast   560
On me. Have I done wrong?

Duchess

Dinarco, you
Are innocent.

Dinarco

I've always tried
To serve you well.

Celso

I too, my lady.
I doubt you can complain of this
Old man. Day in, day out, these windows, doors
And corridors have seen how I
Have carried out my obligations.

Duchess

I know, Celso. And you are blameless.
I respect you as I would my father.

Celso

My tears are the proof of my intentions.

Ruperto
So is Ruperto the guilty man?

Duchess
No, you are not.

Urbino
                    Then that leaves me,
Urbino. It cannot be Antonio you
Are angry with.

Duchess
                    Neither Urbino nor
Ruperto.

Antonio
                    Then I must be the guilty one.
Why won't you speak? Why turn away?
No doubt someone's informed on me.
But even so, you have to listen to
A man who's cared for your house,
Estate, your honour and your son.   580
How can you condemn me out of hand?
But so be it! I'll not defend
Myself against this charge, except
To say that who accuses me
Will surely pay for it!

Duchess
                    How dare
You answer me like this! You have
Dishonoured my good name! I know
Exactly what you've done, and now
You'll pay for it. You'll leave my house
At once!

Celso
                    What can the man be guilty of
To make her banish him?

Furio
                    It's very strange.

Duchess

If I refrain from punishing you both,
It is because . . .
(*She approaches him, speaks quietly.*)
                    . . . Antonio, this
Is pure pretence, to satisfy Urbino.
He saw what happened.

Antonio (*quietly*)

                    I know. It was
Unfortunate. This is a sensible
Solution.

Duchess (*aloud*)

            You'll leave my service now!
(*Quietly.*) But now you also take with you
My happiness. My heart, banished
From joy, will surely die! (*Aloud.*) Go at once,   600
Before I have you put to death.

Antonio (*aloud*)

                    Heaven knows
That I am innocent of any crime!
(*Quietly.*) Leaving you, my heart is full of fear.

Duchess (*quietly*)

Don't be afraid! We'll meet in secret.

Antonio (*aloud*)

I know you'll not forgive me, and so
I'll say no more . . . (*Quietly.*) except to say how much
I love you. I took our daughter away
From here and, by a stroke of luck,
Discovered that the girl who nursed
Our son had given birth six days
Ago, but lost the child . . .

Duchess (*aloud*)

                    There is no more
To say. Leave now! (*Quietly.*) She lost the child?

Antonio (*quietly*)

But then found comfort in our daughter.

Duchess (*quietly*)
    May God bless them! Despite my brothers, you
    Are mine. But say no more.

Antonio (*aloud*)
                                I'll simply say
    You took a villain's word and have
    Dishonoured me on that account.
    But what could I expect from such a woman?

Duchess
    Filelfo, settle up with him.
    Urbino, come with me. And you,   620
    Antonio, do not speak of this, for if
    You do, I'll have your life.

Antonio
                                I'll not
    Say anything, no matter what I feel.

Duchess
    Be grateful you are spared!

Exit the **Duchess**.

Urbino
    Antonio gets what he deserves,
    And in his absence I am honoured.
    Was I, deceived by him, supposed
    To cover up his own deception?
    My loyalty is to the Duchess, not
    To someone who has been disloyal.

Exit **Urbino**.

Furio
    Antonio, it saddens me that such
    A reputable man should cause
    The Duchess such displeasure.

Antonio
    The accusations are entirely false.

Filelfo

In any case, act prudently.
I cannot say if you've done wrong.
Her anger may be temporary.

Dinarco

I too regret all this, Antonio.
But, more than that, my anger is
Towards Urbino. He's always envied you.   640

Antonio

So much, he's engineered this.

Celso

A rogue and villain! Your success
Is what he most resents. But this
Is also due to female fickleness.
Be patient for a while.

Antonio

                    Of course.
I shall resist this childishness.
You know how loyally I served
The king of Naples. He paid me due
Respect. He never thought to throw
Me out, as she has done. It goes to show
We are the playthings of the powerful.

Celso

We live in fear, all of us.

Antonio

And of myself, no doubt, suspicious.

Exit all; enter **Ottavio** *and* **Fabricio**, *ready to go hunting.*

Ottavio

I'll take the Spanish stallion. Have
Him saddled.

Fabricio

                    A splendid animal!
In ancient times he would have pulled

The chariot of the sun. Which harness will
You have?

Ottavio
> I think the scarlet and silver.

Fabricio
My lord, would you have them call you
The love-sick hunter? Green is much   660
More suited to the chase.

Ottavio
> But since
My hopes in love do not exist,
It's far less suited to me, Fabricio.
I've attended the Duchess for three
Long years, and still she spurns me.

Fabricio
> And still
You persist, my lord, in spite of that.

Ottavio
What else am I to do if I was born
To love this woman? For me she is
Divinity itself, the angel I adore,
A Circe who entices me
And then destroys my dreams. Perhaps
The hunt will help me think of other things,
Scatter my foolish thoughts upon
The wind. If only I could leave them there,
Return without them and be at peace.

Fabricio
On the question of giving up hope,
My lord, a wise man once made this
Comparison. Imagine wasps stinging
Your arm. You brush them off, but they
Return much more insistently.   680
A man who has no hope in love
Is much the same. He casts aside

His pain, but it returns to hurt
Him even more.

Ottavio
                    Indeed, Fabricio.
The more I try to cast aside
My grief, the more it wounds me.

Enter **Urbino**.

Urbino
Off hunting, then?

Ottavio
                    I am.

Urbino
                              But not
With much pleasure.

Ottavio
                         The disillusionment
Of love, and a wise old man's advice.
'Take exercise,' he says, and so
I'm going hunting with Fabricio.

Urbino
Well, exercise is good. It takes
One's mind off things.

Ottavio
                              What news, then, of
The cruel angel?

Urbino
                         She's extremely angry.
So much so, she's taken to her room.

Ottavio
You know the cause?

Urbino
                         Household affairs.
The slightest upset sets her off.

Ottavio
I hope it's nothing to do with me.

Urbino
No, not at all. Her steward's to blame.

Ottavio
Impossible! I'd just as well believe   700
There are lions in Spain, or snow in Egypt.

Urbino
The fact is that she's called him to account,
And every effort on his part
To find some reason for delay
Has proved quite useless. In the end
He's been dismissed. No longer is
He her faithful steward.

Ottavio
                              Dismissed,
You say? But why?

Urbino
                        I know the cause
But cannot say.

Ottavio
                      Why not? I have
To know.

Urbino
              Upon my honour as
A gentleman, I cannot say.
It's quite impossible.

Ottavio
                           Then I
Must count for little in your estimation,
Despite my rank. Fabricio, leave us.

Exit **Fabricio**.
So now we are alone, what happened?

Urbino

I find the matter difficult.

Ottavio

Urbino, you are driving me mad.

Urbino

Then, as a man of honour, you
Must swear you'll keep this to yourself.
Not only is the matter most   720
Unfortunate; others are involved.
And just because the two of us
Are friends does not give me the right . . .

Ottavio

I shan't tell a soul!

Urbino

         Very well.
Last night – the clock had just struck one –
I took a walk outside and suddenly
Saw Livia opening a door. She called
To me: 'Antonio.' I went to speak
To her, but then she thrust a baby in
My arms and left. She evidently thought
I was Antonio. Not only did she speak
His name, but he himself appeared as
I held the child. I gave it him at once,
Accused him of betraying me,
And, since I am a loyal servant in
This house, informed the Duchess.

Ottavio

Whose child do you think it is?

Urbino

         Why, Livia's.

Ottavio

Oh, yes, I'm sure! Don't be absurd!

Urbino

Then whose?

Ottavio

        Two months confined to bed!
A good excuse to hide her pregnancy.   740
I'd say the Duchess has a secret lover!

Urbino

Impossible! To entertain a lover here
Would be quite mad. As for Antonio,
She almost had him put to death.

Ottavio

Appearances can be deceptive.

Urbino

I think my own suspicions are
Much nearer the mark. Livia is
Antonio's lover. As for the Duchess, she's
Dismissed him, called him to account,
Disgraced him publicly. And now,
Upset by this, she's taken to her room.
Antonio cannot be her lover.

Ottavio

Secluded she may be, but nuns
Are rarely what they seem. To be
Quite frank, the Devil cannot rival them
For sheer cunning. As I am standing here,
The Duchess has produced a child.

Urbino

By whom?

Ottavio

      Not by some ghost, quite clearly.
She may have seemed to be in mourning, but
A woman, like a field, will not   760
Bear fruit without some careful husbandry.

Urbino

If this were true of her, nothing
Would make me happier, in spite
Of her disgrace. But even so . . .

Ottavio

The guilt is clear.

Urbino

But if it is
Antonio, why dismiss him?

Ottavio

What better way
To cover up? We thought he spent
The time with her arranging her
Affairs. I can see how close they must
Have been! Inform her brothers.

Urbino

Where are
You going?

Ottavio

Where I can vent my anguish
To the hills, the fields, the sky. I thought
It was enough to die of love,
But now I die of infamy. I curse
The day that I set eyes on her,
And, dazzled by her beauty, fell
In love with her. I thought that in
The mountains I would voice complaints
Of unrequited love. But now
I'll only speak of outrage, of   780
This life soon ended. My only wish
Is that these hills should swallow me,
Or that my horse should fall and crush
The life from me! They then can bear
Me lifeless to the Duchess.

Exit **Ottavio**.

Urbino
There is a tale about a king
Who waged a war in Africa
And then went home, unscathed.
A story of a tree whose trunk
A flash of lightning just missed.
A bull who tried to gore a man
But only caught his clothing on its horns.
A ship which found the safety of a port
Though it had sailed along a hostile shore.
A blaze that burned the palace of a king
But spared the cottage of a humble man.
And hail that lashed the countryside
But left the wheat untouched.
And so, just as the king, the tree,
The humble man, the ship, the wheat,   800
Survived to fight another day,
So do my hopes remain alive
For better things ahead.

Act Three

Enter **Antonio** *and* **Bernardo**.

Bernardo
> Continue with the story. It's quite
> Incredible.

Antonio
>   Well, as I've said,
> She thought it more effective if
> I were dismissed, and so I spent
> Six years in all in Naples and Ancona.
> But even so, since nothing was
> Suspected afterwards, I saw
> Her frequently, travelling at night
> And entering a door that Livia opened
> To let me in. Our love is as it was,
> Her beauty my delight. But now
> She's pregnant once again and thinks
> That everyone should be informed
> Of our love and our marriage.
> But now, before she takes this step,
> She's made a visit to Loretto, so
> Escaping Ottavio's fierce jealousy.
> She's left her eldest son in charge
> Of her estates. I do believe
> It's turned out better than we planned.

20

Bernardo
> She's left the palace and her subjects?

Antonio
> You know that absence makes the heart
> Grow fonder. She also fears for
> Her pregnancy. And so, pretending that
> She longs to see Ancona, I'm
> Expecting her this very day.
> Love conquers all, they say, and so

She'll claim she wants to be with me,
The husband whom she values more
Than any kingdom. When all the people learn
Of our unequal match, at least
They'll know our marriage has
Been blessed by heaven.

Bernardo

                    Her brothers will
Go mad. They'll hunt you down.

Antonio

Quite possibly. But pity for
Their nephews ought to blunt their swords,
And noble feelings fill their hearts.
A shepherd brings my children here
Today, eight years away from both
Their parents.

Bernardo

                    The brothers are the worst   40
Of men. I fear for your safety.

Antonio

I know that they are powerful men,
But surely they have gentle feelings too,
Not least when it concerns their family.

Bernardo

Let's hope that heaven can soften all
Desire for revenge.

Enter **Lucindo**.

Lucindo

                    Good news,
My lord.

Antonio

                    The Duchess has arrived?

Lucindo

Indeed she has.

Antonio
                    Then no one could
Be happier than I. Such joy
Will more than compensate for any death.
No matter what the brothers do,
This prize, this crown is all that I
Desire. What nobleman could ask
For more?

Bernardo
                    My friend, the prize
Is great, the danger even greater.

Antonio
If we can live together for
A single hour, man and wife, I swear
I'll die a happy man. Let's go
And welcome them. The children shall
Come too. If they can look at her   60
And not be dazzled by her beauty,
She'll know at once that they are hers.

Exit **Antonio**, **Bernardo** *and* **Lucindo**. *Enter the* **Duchess**,
Livia, **Urbino**, **Celso**, **Furio**, **Dinarco**, *and* **Filelfo**.

Urbino
My lady, why this visit to Antonio?

Duchess
It is intended as a sign of my
Forgiveness.

Urbino
                    I find it strange.
He left your house six years ago,
A man who should have managed your
Affairs but only brought disgrace.
And now you choose to stay with him!
Are other gentlemen in short supply?

Duchess
Far better, I think, the ones we know.

Urbino
Antonio is, of course, extremely poor.

Duchess
But not so poor he cannot offer me
His table and a bed.

Urbino
It seems
I can say nothing right today.

Duchess
Urbino, this is what I wish to do.

Enter **Antonio** *and* **Doristo**. *They are accompanied by*
Antonio's *children:* **Alejandro** *and* **Leonora**, *both in peasant*
dress.

Antonio
My lady, your presence honours
This humble house.

Duchess
My dear Antonio!

Dinarco
This is enough to try one's patience!

Furio
Be quiet! Antonio is a man   80
Of honour and nobility.

Antonio
Allow me to kiss your hand.

Duchess
No, stay!
In future we'll conduct things differently.

Antonio
Then let me present these children,
Two perfect angels.

Duchess
Who are they? Tell

Me.

Doristo
Both mine, my lady.

Antonio
                              Perhaps
You could give them your blessing.
Children, kiss the lady's hand.

Alejandro
I think I love this lady. As soon as
I saw her.

Leonora
                    I think I do as well.

Duchess
So do you have a mother?

Alejandro
                              Our mother's dead.

Doristo
Taken before her proper time she was.

Duchess
And what are you called, my little one?

Alejandro
I'm Alejandro.

Leonora
                    And I'm Leonora.

Duchess (*aside*)
I feel both love and fear. But why
Wait longer? Why have I come if not
To act with resolution? The moment has
Arrived when I must speak. (*Aloud.*) Attend
Me everyone! You all should know
The reason for my visit here.   100
And if I have concealed it from
You previously – for far too long –

I did so in anticipation of today.

Urbino (*aside*)
What is it she intends to say?

Dinarco
My lady, you confuse us all
With this preamble. Please proceed.

Duchess
You know that, when my husband died, I was
Still young, and also had a son
Too young to govern my estates.
Because of that I brought Antonio back
From Naples, making him my steward.
He is, as you all know, a man
Of many qualities. And so it was
That I, observing him, soon came
To fall in love with him. But if
You think this strange, dismiss the thought.
Why, history is full of such examples.
And you should know as well that our love
Was honest and beyond reproach.
Antonio and I were married secretly,   120
And afterwards these children you
See here were born – to me, not Livia,
As many thought. Both of them were raised
By others, far away from us,
And when my little girl was born,
The circumstances led me to dismiss
Antonio from my service. His exile, as
You know, has been the cause of much
Confusion. My eyes are tired of weeping;
The years begin to weigh on me;
My brothers suspect my innocence;
My honour seems in doubt. And so,
To put an end to it, I'm here
Today, and here I now intend
To live. Antonio is my husband.
I want no title, lands, revenues or vassals.

The kingdom of Amalfi has an heir,
My eldest son. He's now a man
And able to govern properly.
He will defend his people and, when   140
He marries, give them a successor to
Himself. Those of you who wish to serve
My son may go with money and with letters.
And those who wish to stay with me
Will have this roof and my affection.

Urbino
So who responds to this?

Furio
               I don't
Know what to say.

Urbino
            You, give your answer!

Dinarco
I cannot. Let the oldest speak.

Celso
I am the oldest. It seems to me
That what is done is done and cannot be
Undone. Because of that, advice
Is useless. Of course, the matter will
Occasion gossip, give your brothers food
For thought, and bring much sorrow to
Your subjects. May God bring peace of mind
To all of them, as I am sure He will,
For, as you say, this marriage has been blessed
By God himself. Now as for me,
I held you in my arms when you
Were one year old, and so I could   160
Not leave you now. In any case, I
Am old and willing to accept
Whatever blow or pardon comes to me
For being at your side. I'll serve
Antonio. His merits are well known,

Enhanced by your choosing him
As your husband.

Duchess

         Be of good cheer, Celso.
I do believe my brothers will
Be moved by our common blood,
My children's tender years, and by
Antonio's qualities of mind
And spirit. Furio, why so silent?

Furio

Simply because I did not wish
To tell you what I feel. To be
Quite frank, I feared it would come
To this. Your eyes could not conceal
The secrets of your heart. And so,
Forgive me when I say I am
Obliged to leave. I have decided I
Shall serve your son and thus respect   180
The Duke, his father, whom you've wronged.

Exit **Furio**.

Dinarco

My lady, there are reasons why
I have to leave you too, not least
Because of all the dangers that
You face. May God protect you. As for
Myself, old age obliges me
To seek some safer place.

Exit **Dinarco**.

Filelfo

If things were different here, I'd stay,
But everything has gone too far.
I fail to understand it all.
I beg permission to depart.
I wish you well.

Duchess

           My friend, I'm grateful that
You choose to serve my son.

Filelfo

            For reasons I
Have given. May God be with you!

Exit **Filelfo**.

Urbino

I too could leave, but I condemn
Them all. I'll serve Antonio as
I've served yourself. If he deserves
To be your husband, he shall be
My master too. I know I have
Offended him, so now I beg   200
Forgiveness.

Antonio

          Come along, Urbino.
I've always seen you as a friend
And brother.

Duchess

         And I'm indebted to
Your love. I trust, upon my husband's life,
My gratitude can be its equal.

Urbino

Your excellency . . .

Duchess

           No titles, please.
Amalfi has its duke. I wish
To be exactly what Antonio is.
No lands or life of luxury.
His wife, no more. You, Livia, shall
Be married to Urbino. I may
Be poor but I still have the means
To offer you a dowry.

Livia
To serve

You is a dowry in itself.
I'd offer up my life if there
Were need of it.

Duchess
Doristo, you

Have been a good and worthy man.
I want you here with me, so you
Must change these clothes.

Doristo
I shall,

My lady, and you should know how much   220
This pleases me. I couldn't leave
These little angels. Although they beat
Me to a pulp and treat me like
A dog, I'd die for them.

Duchess
They too

Must change their clothes.

Antonio
Indeed

They must. The whole world knows that they
Are yours.

Duchess
Come, then. We share the things

We have, though wealth is of the least
Importance. Our house shall be humble,
Our clothes modest. But in our love we
Shall be most royal.

Antonio
My joy is such,

My tears choke my words.

They exit. Enter **Julio de Aragon** *and* **Ottavio de Medici**.

Julio

If my brother knew of this, his sword
Would lose no time in piercing
The villain's heart.

Ottavio

What she has done
Is worse than anything committed by
A noble woman. A servant in her bed!

Julio

As well as young and shameless, she
Is clearly mad.

Ottavio

Antonio may well be
A man of noble qualities, but he   240
Can never be her equal.

Julio

A commoner,
And now our brother-in-law. Enough
To drive one mad! No doubt she loves
This dog, but why not keep it secret,
Indulge her lust behind closed doors?
But no! She openly proclaims
This marriage, leaves her home,
Her son, her lands, and so demeans
The honour of our family.
By God, this is a crime that has
To be avenged, and I shall see
To it before the Cardinal,
My brother, is informed. Why should
The Duke, our nephew, have this vile
Antonio for a father? I cannot bear
The thought of it!

Ottavio

Nor I. I am
A man of honour, a true Medici!
Her suitor too! Such infamy

Has cut me to the quick, and so
I am resolved on sweet revenge.   260
However safe they think Ancona is,
It is not short of guns or knives
For hire. In any case, I'd willingly put
An end to him myself!

Julio
                   Why, servants can
Do that, Ottavio. The more I think of it,
It angers me that those poor children live
Beneath the shadow of such infamy.

Ottavio
Both raised by peasants far away
From here.

Julio
              Brother and sister to a duke!
How inappropriate! Let's go, Ottavio.
Oh, treacherous sister! Vengeance shall
Be mine!

Ottavio
            Oh, sweet Duchess! How sad
Antonio has to die!

Exit **Julio** *and* **Ottavio**. *Enter the* **Duke of Amalfi**, *son of the* **Duchess**, **Furio**, **Dinarco**, *and* **Filelfo**.

Duke
It seems the Cardinal and all
My relatives already know.

Furio
And they condemn such aberration in
A woman of such noble birth.

Duke
How could my mother do this thing?
An act of madness that destroys
The reputation of our family!   280

How is it that her love of me
Could not restrain her? She loved
Antonio more! If only I had died
At birth!

Filelfo

Do not give way to grief,
My lord!

Duke

Say that, you cannot know
What honour is. Eight years this infamy
Has been concealed.

Dinarco

Some hinted at
The truth, then thought it best to hold
Their tongues. There were, as well, some signs.
Ottavio often spoke his mind,
But no one listened. The virtues which
The Duchess had convinced them he
Was wrong.

Duke

Virtues as false as any make-up!
So must I think I am Antonio's son?

Furio

Of course not, sir. A father is
The person who gives life, not someone who
Has merely raised a child. He is
No more than your stepfather.

Duke

It seems my mother has displayed
A woman's frailty. What more is there   300
To say? If she had any real thought
For me, she would have shown me more
Consideration, not demeaned
Me in this way. But why should I
Require such attention? Let her give

It to Antonio's children. She chose
To marry him, lowly as the marriage is.

Filelfo

Do not give way to jealousy, my lord!

Duke

I promise you, I am not jealous.
Why, if I had those children here,
I'd love them as a true brother.
In any case, they aren't as low-born as
We think. Antonio is a gentleman,
Albeit poor. And so I think I'll give
Them money from my mother's property
To supplement Antonio's. Inform
My uncles. Give Antonio proper praise.

Dinarco

The world was blessed the day that you
Were born.

Duke

We must be brave, play down
These misdemeanours. Say good things   320
Of him. This, certainly, is my
Intention.

Furio

On their behalf, our grateful thanks.

Duke

Now hear me well. Let no one say
A word against Antonio.

Furio

You have
A truly noble heart, my lord.

Duke

We also need to help my mother.
What did she take with her?

Dinarco
> Only
> Her silver, jewels, clothes, and bedding.

Duke
> What? Nothing more?

Dinarco
> No, only that.

Duke
> Then she has given all for love.
> Twenty-five thousand ducats for them
> To set up house. If needs be, we
> Shall borrow it.

Furio
> Your generosity, my lord,
> Exceeds all bounds.

Duke
> Five thousand for
> My brother and sister. They need to dress
> As is appropriate. So let's inform
> Our subjects that Antonio is to be
> Respected. Indeed, he shall be known
> As 'Signor Antonio', honest husband that
> He is. As for my mother, she is moved   340
> By love, as women tend to be. So who
> Can blame her?

Exit all. Enter the **Duchess**, **Antonio**, *and* **Urbino**.

Urbino
> It's best you flee as soon
> As possible. They're on their way,
> And thirsting for revenge. Remember what
> I told you in Ancona.

Duchess
> My flesh and blood!
> They have no pity! Why? What do

They want?

Antonio

They want me dead!

Duchess

But there
Are other reasons for compassion. Don't
You see?

Antonio

We'll make for Venice. We'll be
Much safer. I know the Republic will grant
Me favours.

Urbino

Then best be on your way.

Duchess

My children. I cannot go without them.

Urbino

They are coming now.

Enter **Livia** *and the children.*

Livia

You need to hurry. Someone's told
Me there are soldiers in the wood.
They can't know what you plan to do,
So you should leave at once.

Duchess

We had
To wait until the children came.

Enter **Celso**.

Celso

Leave now! We came across a spy.
No sooner did he spot us than he ran   360
Away.

Antonio
> On foot or horseback?

Celso
> On foot,
> But armed.

Enter **Doristo**, *dressed as a squire.*

Doristo
> Soldiers, my lord, and moving fast
> In this direction.

Duchess
> Antonio, you
> Should leave. It's you my brother wants,
> Not me. I know I shall be safe.

Doristo
> Although I was a peasant yesterday,
> My lord, I know what honour is,
> And cowardice too. To flee from here
> Is not to be a coward.

Antonio
> But can't
> You see? To leave my wife is worse
> Than death.

Celso
> Take this old man's advice.
> Go now. No need to be concerned.
> Urbino and I are here.

Duchess
> Far better than
> To stay and have your wife without
> A husband, your children without
> A father.

Alejandro
> Please, father. Do what mother asks.
> Don't die!

Leonora

Why are you waiting?

Antonio

Because
I want to protect you, child.

Leonora

Then we'll
All die.

Antonio

Then never think that I'm
A coward! God be with you! Embrace me!   380
Accept these tears! And you, my one
And only love, forgive me! Goodbye,
Urbino, Doristo, Livia, Celso.

Duchess

My thoughts go with you.

Exit **Antonio**.

Children, I need
You with me.

Leonora

Is father gone, for ever
And ever?

Duchess

I cannot say. Fate's never been kind.

Alejandro

I could speak to uncle, mother. He is
A cardinal.

Duchess

No, no, he's turned
His back on us.

Alejandro

If I were big enough,
I'd challenge Uncle Julio to a duel.

Duchess
Now only heaven protects us.

Leonora
God
Will help us, I know He will.

Enter **Julio de Aragon** *and* **Ottavio**, *accompanied by four
servants with harquebuses and halberds.*

Ottavio
Well, here they are.

Julio
Let no one move!
All of you, vile, immoral cowards!
Stay where you are!

Duchess
Brother, no one
Is trying to escape.

Julio
You dare to call
Me brother? Is that what you think
I am, you whore?

Duchess
So are you not Julio
De Aragon?

Julio
Of course.

Duchess
Then am
I not your sister?

Julio
No, you are not!   400
The Duchess of Amalfi is already dead.
She *was* my sister!

Duchess

And still is!

Julio

Do you hear, Ottavio? She shows true wit.
The wife of Antonio de Bolonia.
She claims to be my sister, pretends
She is the Duchess of Amalfi.

Ottavio

The Duchess of Amalfi would not
Have thought of anything so vile,
Much less indulged in it.

Duchess

And you,
Why are you here?

Ottavio

Why not?

Duchess

You have
No business with our family. Aren't you
A Medici?

Ottavio

Indeed! And we can count
Both kings and popes among our numbers.

Duchess

But nothing to do with the Aragons.
You do not share our blood.

Ottavio

Except
For friendship, the noblest kind
Of blood, the source of true honour.

Duchess

Is that the true extent of your love?

Ottavio

No, it is not. My love survives until
Its cause does not.

Duchess

                    You, Julio, what   420
Do you want of me?

Julio

                    Whose children are they?

Duchess

Why, mine, of course, and your niece
And nephew.

Julio

                    I have one nephew, only one:
The Duke of Amalfi, the son
Of someone who shared our blood
And so was our equal.

Duchess

                    These are
The son and daughter of a man
Whose virtue and intelligence has
No equal. If you deny that they
Are your niece and nephew, remember they
Are still my children. And if they lack
A father, heaven must do, for heaven protects all
Those whom men despise.

Julio

Heaven also punishes those who sin.

Duchess

I married according to heaven's will.

Julio

No, you offended it.

Duchess

                    Not to be married would
Have been the true offence.

Julio

                You could
Have kept our shame a secret.

Duchess

                     What shame
If I am married?

Ottavio

            There is no point
In arguing.

Duchess

         Since when did jealousy   440
Speak well of love?

Ottavio

              I am not jealous; I
Am wronged!

Duchess

           How wronged if I
Was never yours?

Ottavio

            You wrongly kept
My hopes alive.

Duchess

           I think your hopes
Were mere presumption.

Julio

                No matter! Where's
Your husband, the one they call Signor
Antonio?

Duchess

          Certainly not here. He's in
Milan.

Julio

       You mean he didn't come

With you?

Duchess
          He'd heard of all your cruelties.

Julio
Ah, well, the Cardinal and I
Have friends in many places. You'll come
With us.

Duchess
          Am I a prisoner?

Julio
                    You are
Indeed!

Duchess
          But why? I've done no wrong.

Julio
You think dishonouring the house
Of Aragon is right?

Duchess
                    On whose authority
Am I a prisoner? The King or Pope?

Julio
You'll come with us. So, who are you?

Urbino
Her secretary, sir.

Julio
                    Why have you left
The Duke?

Urbino
          I've never served
The Duke. Only my lady.

Julio
                    And you?   460

Celso
>A loyal servant, sir. I've served
>Her well for fourteen years.

Julio
>   You there?

Doristo
>I cared for both her children. Why, yesterday
>I was a shepherd, had a flock of sheep.
>And here I am, a courtier,
>And witness only to misfortune.

Julio
>It seems, Ottavio, that our man
>Was warned.

Ottavio
>   Urbino, were you part
>Of this wrongdoing?

Urbino
>   I cannot see
>It's wrong to marry, sir.

Ottavio
>   Not when
>A woman has offended men of true
>Nobility?

Julio
>   Leave that for now.
>The Duchess and the children are
>Our only interest. The rest of you
>Are free to go.

Duchess
>   But why the children?
>They have done nothing wrong.

Alejandro
>   Are we
>Your prisoners, uncle?

Julio

              I am not
Your uncle, boy. Don't be impertinent!
We leave for Amalfi.

Duchess

                It doesn't matter what
Becomes of me. Kill me if you wish.   480
As long as my Antonio lives!

Exit all. Enter **Antonio**.

Antonio

What am I doing, fleeing shamefully,
Abandoning the life I had through fear
Of death? I've left the woman I
Adore in their hands, my children too.
Oh, this is hard to bear! The wife
I worship, Alejandro, Leonora,
A third as yet unborn. The man
Who comes to this from such a state
Of happiness must break his heart.
What is there left of life when I
Am forced to think of what I've lost?
The rocks below are tempting me
To end it all. This sword, this knife,
How easy it would be! Not least
If those I love have perished at
The hands of heartless men! Oh, why
Is it I do not kill myself? I have
No place to go, no life to live without
My children and my dearest wife.   500

Enter **Doristo**.

Doristo

Damn all these paths! I think I'm lost.
But, being lost, look who I've found.
Signor Antonio!

Antonio

Is that you, Doristo?
Have you escaped, abandoned all
My precious ones? I want to know
If they are dead.

Doristo

By no means dead,
My lord. They're in Amalfi with the Duke.
The Duchess was received most warmly.
The Duke rode out to welcome her.
I saw them laughing together,
Enjoying each other's company.
The Duke embraced his brother and sister
And asked his mother about your marriage.
Then her brother Julio said that he
Was truly sorry you weren't there.
So, as you see, the Duke is pleased
And, being so, intends to look on you
More kindly. This letter's from Urbino.

Antonio

Oh, this is such good news! Are you
Quite sure it's turned out well?

Doristo

I saw   520
It for myself, my lord. With these
Two eyes, as true as I am standing here.

Antonio

Heaven has been moved to pity me.
I must accept this happiness
With much more calm than past misfortunes.

(*He reads the letter.*) 'Things have turned out quite differently
from how we thought they would. The Duke has proved
himself an angel of peace against the wrath of Julio de Aragon
and Ottavio de Medici. Don't go too far away, keep abreast
of what is happening. I trust in God that He will give you
peace of mind and body quite soon. Urbino Castelvetro.'

This letter is the very source
Of life. It has revived my hopes.
Oh, let these tears be its due reward
Until I can provide for it
A casket made of gold and pearls.
So is it true, Doristo, that
The Duke now favours me?

Doristo
He's calmed his uncle's rage, and that   540
Of others. He also makes a fuss
Both of the Duchess and the children.

Enter **Urbino**.

Urbino
I'll never find him in this wilderness.
I've left my horse for dead and now
I've lost my way.

Antonio
                          There's someone there!

Urbino
What's that? Footsteps! My God, is that
Antonio?

Antonio
                My eyes must be deceiving me!
It's surely Urbino.

Doristo
                        If that's him,
He wants to take you to Amalfi.

Antonio
Urbino! What news?

Urbino
                            This is a miracle.
I came to look for you and, having lost
My way, I end up finding you.

Antonio
Why look for me?

Urbino
To ask you to come back.

Antonio
But why?

Urbino
The Duke has smoothed the way,
Has acted like the prince he is,
And pacified his uncles. Rest
Assured! Julio's had a change of heart.
His brother has instructed him
That you must not be harmed – indeed,
That you be treated with respect.   560
The Cardinal regards you as a man
Of some importance. He favours you.
And Julio's asked me to give you this.

He hands **Antonio** *a letter.*

Antonio
In short, he shows true magnanimity.

Urbino
We have to leave at once.

Antonio
You are
Quite sure all is well?

Urbino
Of course!

Antonio (*reads*) 'The Cardinal, my brother, has informed me
that you, your wife and children must be left in peace. The
one condition is that you now agree to live in Spain or
Germany. In this case you may come and take them with
you.'

Spain or Germany? To be

Together, I'd take them anywhere.
Urbino, my grateful thanks. You see,
Heaven pities me at last.

Urbino
                              I think
I well deserve your thanks. Let's go!
The Duchess awaits.

Antonio
                              If only horses
Had wings!

Doristo
                    I'll be your guide, my lord.

Urbino
Then hurry we shall!

Exit all. Enter **Ottavio,** **Julio,** *and the* **Duke**.

Duke
I am indebted, uncle. For this   580
I shall be grateful all my life.

Julio
If you are happy, nephew, others will
Be happy too.

Ottavio
                    Then no more talk
About the past. What matters is
A cure for past ills. The Duke
Should help his mother prepare to leave.

Duke
If only I could, I'd give her my
Inheritance complete. But since I am
Obliged, as son and heir, to keep
These lands, I'll give her all the rest.
It saddens me she has to leave.

Julio

> The Duchess can never return
> To Italy.

Duke

>   If that is your wish,
> So be it.

Julio (*taking* **Ottavio** *aside*)

>   Ottavio . . .

Ottavio

>   What is it?

Julio

>   No need
> For you to worry any more.
> The Duchess has received just payment for
> The damage to our family name.
> The meal was her reward.

Ottavio

>   The meal?

Julio

> In less than half an hour she'll
> Be dead.

Ottavio

>   Oh, no, what have you done?   600
> This is unfair, unjust!

Julio

>   Ottavio,
> Her crime is unforgivable!

Ottavio

> You know I loved her, adored her!
> It's more than I can bear!

Julio

>   Control
> Yourself! The Duke will hear us.

Ottavio
The woman is a perfect angel
This can't be right!

Julio
      Be silent or
I shall forget myself. How can
An angel so offend our name
For mere lust?

Ottavio
      But this is madness!

Duke
Why is Ottavio so upset?
I thought that everyone was now
At peace.

Julio
     He thinks we ought to let
Your mother stay.

Duke
       I'd like that more
Than anything.

Julio
      Then she can stay,
For your sake.

Duke
     God bless you, uncle.

Enter **Urbino**, **Antonio**, *and* **Doristo**.

Antonio
I've never felt such fear as this.

Urbino
My lord, this is Antonio.

Antonio
       I bow
Before you. I once believed I was

Important. In your presence all   620
I feel is true humility.

Duke

Antonio, my mother gives you to
Me as a father. As such I see
You now and always.

Antonio

I am unworthy of
That name. Much better if I kneel
At your feet.

Duke

Not so, Antonio.
If God has blessed your marriage, I
Am your son. My mother gave
Me life. She's given you nobility.
My wishes are the same as hers.
I value what she values most.

Antonio

Such generosity allows me to
Believe that things are better than
I'd hoped.

Duke

Come, greet my uncle. He
Has shown great mercy.

Antonio

I beg you, plead
My cause with all these powerful men.

Duke

Uncle, this is Antonio.

Julio

I know
Exactly who he is. I'll speak
With him.

Duke
>Please, treat him kindly.

Antonio
>My lord, if I've offended you,   640
>I now apologise.

Julio (*aside*)
>   God give me patience!
>(*Aloud.*) Antonio, the Cardinal and I
>Are both agreed that you should keep
>Your wife. But now you should get ready to
>Depart. We've placed this room at your disposal.

Antonio
>My lord, I am most grateful.

Julio
>   No need
>To thank me. Your wife awaits.

Antonio
>   May heaven
>Repay you for this favour!

Duke
>   Uncle, this
>Is true compassion.

Antonio
>   Damn the step!

Julio
>What's that?

Ottavio
>   Antonio, he almost fell.

Julio
>Distracted, no doubt, by thoughts of pleasure.

Antonio
>Please God this doesn't point to more
>Misfortune!

Exit **Antonio**.

Ottavio

          I can't believe
I've had a hand in this. I shall go mad!
But here's the Duchess. She looks quite well.
It could well be that Julio's lied
About the poison.

Enter the **Duchess** *and* **Livia**.

Duchess

               Can this be true?

Livia

    It's what I've heard.

Duchess

                 I've come to see
Antonio. They say he's here.

Duke

                     You didn't see
Him?

Livia

    Perhaps they lied.

Duke

                 He went inside.   660
You must have passed each other.

Enter **Fenicio**, **Julio**'s *servant*.

Fenicio

    It's all been seen to, sir.

Julio (*to the* **Duchess**)

                So, you didn't see him?

Duchess

    No. Please send a page to look for him.

Duke

    At once! Have my father summoned.

Julio

How can you call him father when
He has disgraced your mother?

Duke

I thought
This matter was now forgotten.

Julio

Indeed
It is. We need to bury it, once and for all.
Now, sister, you shall see your children and
The man who dared to call you wife.
Let's open the doors and gaze upon
A sight that surely would please
The Cardinal and also give the Duke
Some joy. As for yourself, good sister,
Prepare to die. The poison will soon
Complete its task. Open the doors!

The doors are opened. Inside is a table on which there are three plates.
Antonio's *head is placed on the middle plate, and on those to either*
side the heads of the two children.

Duchess

Oh, God! What monster has done this?
Deceived me with honeyed words and killed
My husband and my children! May God
Avenge this treachery! Cry out,   680
My children! Oh, angels in heaven, plead
For these earthly creatures! God grant
Me justice! Alejandro, Leonora,
My little ones! Antonio, beloved husband!
My very soul!

Julio

The poison works!
She falls!

Ottavio

Is this reality or are

My eyes deceiving me? Ah, heaven,
If you have eyes, why are you blind to this?
If you have ears, why are you deaf?
This life of mine is meaningless!

Julio

Ottavio, control yourself!

Ottavio

What for?
I have no hope.

Julio

Why throw your cloak away?

Ottavio

The woman I loved is dead. There is
No point to my existence. The ship
Is wrecked, so let the sea consume
My worldly wealth!

Ottavio *rushes out.*

Duke

Only a wild
And untamed beast could look upon
This carnage. Draw your sword! Mine
Shall be stained with your blood!

Julio

Why speak
Such childish words? You need to understand   700
That what's been done restores your honour.

Exit **Julio**.

Duke

Vile and merciless creatures!
I swear this sword will never leave
My hand. I swear I'll never dress
In silk or gold, or wear this chain,
Or sit at their table until revenge
Is mine. Lay her body out!

The Capulets and Montagues

A tragicomedy

Lope de Vega

Characters

Roselo, *a Montague*
Julia, *a Capulet*
Arnaldo, *Roselo's father*
Antonio, *Julia's father*
Teobaldo, *Antonio's brother*
Ottavio, *Teobaldo's son*
Dorotea, *Teobaldo's daughter*
Anselmo, *a friend of Roselo*
The Duke of Verona
The Count of Paris
Marín, *Roselo's servant*
Celia, *Julia's servant*
Lidio, *Arnaldo's servant*
Lucio, *Antonio's servant*
Fesenio, *Teobaldo's servant*
Silvia, *a lady*
Fernando, *a suitor*
Rutilio, *Fernando's servant*
Celio, *a young man*
Fabio, *a young man*
Belardo, *a peasant*
Loreto, *Belardo's son*
Tamar, *Belardo's daughter*
A Captain
Ladies, Gentlemen, Soldiers, Musicians, Servants

Act One

Enter **Anselmo, Roselo,** *and* **Marín.**

Anselmo

    The place is alive with laughter and
    Rejoicing.

Roselo

        It looks as if a son
    Or daughter's getting married.

Anselmo

                        I'd say
    For sure a concert or a wedding.

Roselo

    Marín, find out what's going on.

Marín

    And have them give me the last rites?
    These people are your worst enemies.

Roselo

    But no one knows you. It'll be all right.

Marín

    There's always someone looking for trouble.
    The Capulets are dangerous.

Roselo

    Don't tell me you are scared, Marín.

Marín

    Of course I'm not. If they were here
    Outside, armed to the teeth, I'd take
    Them on single-handed. But there
    Inside, what could be more stupid?

Anselmo

    If you want to know what's happening,
    Disguise yourself. Put on a mask.

They'll think you are a relative.

Roselo
You think it'll work?

Anselmo
                    Of course, unless
There's someone wants to know who   20
You really are.

Roselo
                    All right, Anselmo. The two
Of us.

Anselmo
        The place is full of gorgeous women.
It may be dangerous, but that's
What you'd expect when your father's head
Of all the Montagues. The mere mention of
The Capulets drives him insane.
And as for them, Antonio, head
Of their family, is just the same.
He hates the Montagues.

Roselo
                            I reckon fate
Has given both the families
Quite different things. We Montagues
Are blessed, throughout our history,
With brave and valiant men; the Capulets
With women of outstanding beauty.
It seems to me that if both families
Were joined in marriage and set aside
Their mutual hostility, the whole
Of Italy would envy them.

Marín
        Indeed it would. Besides, it's not
Just human beings are affected by   40
This constant animosity.
Why, even the dogs are mortal enemies.

No sooner do they leave the house,
Just watch them snarling, snapping,
Capulets and Montagues alike,
Mongrels and mastiffs baring teeth.
If they were swords or knives, they'd keep
The police in permanent employment.
As well as that, there's not a man
In either family whose dog does not
Possess a collar armed with sharp
And vicious spikes. And what about
The cats? You see them on the roofs,
And in the kitchens too, as if they were
A battleground, their fur on end,
And spitting at each other, the one
Proclaiming 'I'm a Montague',
The other 'I'm a Capulet'. And then
The hens as well. Just listen to them cluck.
If just one Capulet clucks first,   60
Then thirty Montagues respond
In unison. It's quite incredible.

Roselo

Oh, very witty! That's typical
Of your way of thinking!

Marín

                And so
Is this of you behaving foolishly.
You put yourself where all your enemies
Can take revenge for what your family
Has done to them. At least my piece
Was just a bit of fun, intended to amuse.

Roselo

All right, Marín, it's just that we
Are very different characters.
I hate what's possible and love
Those things that seem impossible.
Anselmo, if I deserve your friendship, come
With me. Set common sense aside.

Let's follow our instinct. We'll find
Some clothes, put on our masks, and see
What's going on from where the room
Is darkest. There's such a crowd in there
We shan't be seen.

Anselmo

                Disguise our passport to   80
Success. Quite clearly, the beauty of
These girls inspires you.

Roselo

                I've been
Without it far too long, hence this madness.

Anselmo

Of course.

Marín

            Let's hope it all ends well.

Roselo

Nothing ventured, nothing gained, Marín.
Besides, to taste forbidden fruit
Is always dangerous.

Exit **Roselo**, **Anselmo**, *and* **Marín**. *Enter* **Antonio**,
Teobaldo, **Julia**, **Dorotea**, **Celia**, **Ottavio**, *other ladies,
gentlemen, and musicians.*

Antonio

Much better here. The heat inside's
Unbearable.

Ottavio (*to* **Julia**)

            I find it doesn't matter, cousin.
For me the heat is just the same, inside
Or out.

Julia

          I think you flatter me simply
Because I have no companion.

Ottavio

It's I
Who need your company.

Julia

But there are lots
Of ladies here. I'm sure they'd like
To have you speak to them.

Ottavio

I do
Not wish to.

Julia

You should.

Ottavio

They do not interest me.
My feelings lie where I shall never be
Admitted.

Teobaldo

Let's sit here!

Antonio

Just look at them!
Aren't both our children handsome?

Teobaldo

Indeed
They are. My greatest joy would be   100
To see them married.

Antonio

No reason why
Two cousins can't be. They are so
Well suited.

Enter **Celio** *and* **Fabio**, *masked.*

Celio

Are we allowed to dance?

Antonio
Of course, go right ahead.

Celio
                                        Let's go.

Fabio
What kind of dance?

Celio
My lady has a change of heart.
Her eyes ablaze with love's bright fire,
Pay no attention to her words,
Her eyes reflect her true desire.

Enter **Anselmo**, **Roselo**, *and* **Marín**, *masked.*

Anselmo
Ah, there they are, all wearing masks.

Roselo
Anselmo, not so loud!

Anselmo
                              The dancing must
Have ended. They're all outside.

Roselo
My God! The women look magnificent.
A paradise of female beauty! I shall
Forget the hatred I've been taught
To feel towards the Capulets!

Anselmo
So which do you prefer?

Roselo
                              The one
That lucky fellow's speaking to.

Anselmo
Then speak to her yourself. Be bold!

Roselo
She doesn't seem too pleased with him.   120

Anselmo
Roselo, keep the mask on!

Roselo
                         I wasn't thinking.

Anselmo
Quickly! Put it on!

Roselo
                    There's nothing to hide.
It's fine like this.

Anselmo
                    Too late. They've seen
You already.

Antonio
                What's going on? Roselo!
You dare set foot in here?

Teobaldo (*to* **Antonio**)
                         Antonio, patience!

Antonio
Why must I be patient?

Teobaldo
                         From what
I've heard, the boy is innocent
And good. Because he's young, he feels
No enmity towards your family, as do
His elders. The proof of it lies in
The fact that, knowing what's gone on,
He dares appear here at all.

Antonio
It could well be a trick. He might
Be armed.

Teobaldo
            Antonio, calm yourself.
The boy has come not knowing if
He is in error.

Antonio
            An insult to
My family.

Teobaldo
            No, quite the opposite.
He honours it.

Antonio
            I see it differently.
The boy deserves to die.

Teobaldo
            Then I
Shall not be part of it. It seems   140
To me he's like the bird of prey
Who finds himself amongst a flock
Of doves but has no thought of harming them.
His motives are more innocent.
Forget the feud, Antonio. Do
Not cause a scandal in Verona!

Antonio
You may be right, my friend. You speak
Good sense.

Teobaldo
            It comes with age, Antonio.
Besides, you have a daughter here,
And so do I.

Antonio
            In that case I accept
Your good advice.

Teobaldo
            It's for the best,

Believe me.

Anselmo (*to* **Roselo**)
>What are you looking at?

Roselo
A fatal vision.

Anselmo
>You may be right.
Continue looking and you'll give
These people cause to put an end to you.

Roselo
They seem relaxed enough.

Anselmo
>If you
Don't stop, they might act differently.

Roselo
Anselmo, please! I need to gaze
Upon this perfect angel. Let them do
Their worst. Before we go to heaven,   160
We have to die on earth, as you
Well know. So it is only fair
That I should die.

Anselmo
>I must admit,
She isn't bad.

Roselo
>She isn't bad?
Say exquisite!

Dorotea (*to* **Julia**)
>Why, that young man
Is so good-looking!

Roselo
>Why can't I overcome
My fears and let my passion speak

For me? But still, we are amongst
Our enemies.

Anselmo
                    Indeed! Be careful!

Julia
If Cupid wanted a disguise,
I think he might have borrowed this
Young man's good looks. Perhaps he is
The god of love personified,
Intending to disturb our peace of mind.

Roselo (*aside*)
If only I were born a Capulet
And not a Montague! Why has
My fate been so unfortunate?

Julia (*aside*)
The flowers are so beautiful,
Yet he is brighter than them all.

Roselo (*aside*)
If she is paradise, the women in   180
My family must, in comparison,
Be sheer ugliness! Oh, love, overcome
My fear! Give me courage! I must speak
To her.

Julia (*aside*)
        If only he'd speak to me,
I'd please him more than any of
These other women.

Dorotea (*aside*)
                    While Julia's talking to
My brother, this young man can talk
To me.

Roselo (*aside*)
        Love blinds me but inspires me too!

Julia (*aside*)
Oh, let this be my lucky day!

Dorotea (*aside*)
Oh, let him sit by me!

Julia (*aside*)
Let him sit here!

Dorotea (*aside*)
Oh, let him fall in love with me!

Roselo *sits next to* **Julia**, **Anselmo** *next to* **Dorotea**.

Ottavio (*to* **Julia**)
He's probably disguised as Love
To teach me something of the art
Of love. I expect he thinks I need
Some competition. Oh, never mind!
His passion's pointless anyway.
The coldness in this garden will soon
Put out his fire. In any case, we all
Know love's completely blind.

Roselo
Oh, please forgive me, madam. It's much   200
Too bold of me to sit so close to you.
But you, in fact, are more to blame
For it than I. You see, my boldness stems
From your beauty, for which you are
Yourself to blame, while I am innocent.
The truth is that your beauty beckoned me,
Much as a moth is helplessly
Attracted to a flame. And, like the moth,
I circled timidly at first, and only then
Came closer to the light. You know
How Phaeton drove the chariot of the sun
Until he lost control and died, the victim of
His father's thunderbolt. As he
Was reckless, so am I, burning in
The perfect heaven of your beauty.

But rather this than live a cold
And dreary life. So do not think
That I am over-bold. If beauty is
A flame, it is a flame that burns.
Believe me, what I feel is love,   220
The love for which a mortal man may die,
And so, because of that, I am obliged to speak
Before I die.

Julia

        Such tender sentiments!
And yet I know all this is but an act.

Ottavio

But he's removed the mask. He shouldn't speak
To you like this.

Roselo

        Ottavio, please
Forgive me. Attribute all my boldness to
The character. If this offends you, I
Shall leave.

Ottavio

        A good idea!

Julia

        But why?
If he lacks passion too, he ought to stay.
The two of you deserve each other.
You leave me cold, Ottavio. So cold,
In fact, that I could turn that coldness on to him
And make of him a block of pure ice!

Ottavio

Please, cousin, moderate your words.

Julia

I pay attention to this stranger
Because I do not wish to favour you.

Ottavio
> Perhaps, but that does not imply
> You should offend someone who is
> So close to you. For you to favour me,   240
> I'd willingly become as much a stranger as
> This fellow.

Roselo
>   My lady, if I'm in the wrong,
> I'll go away.

Julia
>   Go where?

Roselo
>   Wherever I
> Can be amused.

Julia
>   But isn't this amusing?

Roselo
> It is. But if I've caused offence . . .

Julia
> The person who deserves a favour does
> Not cause offence. (*To* **Roselo**.) Don't speak!
> I wish to make this fool so angry, he'll
> Decide to leave. (*Aloud.*) Ottavio, please!

Ottavio
> You wish to speak to me when you've
> Already turned your back?

Julia
>   Don't be so
> Quick-tempered! Of course I wish to speak to you.

Ottavio
> Then I am less quick-tempered than I was.

Julia *directs her words to* **Ottavio** *but extends her hand to*
Roselo.

Roselo (*aside*)
  Oh, this hand!

Julia
          I fully intend to make
  You happy.

*While **Julia** faces **Ottavio**, her words are intended for **Roselo**.*

Julia
          Such is the nature of
  My passion, it disregards my honour.
  What else is there to say?

Roselo (*aside*)
              Only that
  The man who wants a drink does not
  Need further invitation!

Julia
              A girl
  Who turns her back surrenders to   260
  Her enemy. Don't you think so?

Ottavio
  When you did that and turned to him
  Instead, I thought it was because
  You hated me.

Julia
          So is that why I give
  Up everything for you?

Ottavio
                  My lady, this
  Is wonderful!

Roselo (*aside*)
          I'd say fantastic!

Julia
  My feelings were so strong, I lost
  Control. I'm sorry I was rude.

Ottavio
I thought it came from being in
This public place.

Julia
                Oh, no. I hope
That you intend to please me.

Ottavio
                          Oh, this
Is paradise!

Roselo (*aside*)
          I'll be in heaven!

Julia
If we were somewhere else, I'd show
You how I feel.

Ottavio
            I dare not think
Such happy thoughts!

Roselo (*aside*)
               Nor I
Absorb such happy words!

Julia
                Such is
The power of love!

Ottavio
             And sweeter still
If one's been treated cruelly.

Roselo (*aside*)
The idiot thinks these words are just
For him.

Julia
          I've never met a man   280
Who pleases me so much.

Ottavio

                             Oh, let
This love consume me totally!

Julia
But never think my love is offered lightly.

Ottavio
Of course not. Love is always serious.

Roselo (*aside to* **Julia**)
I expect you think me over-bold.
The truth is that I fell in love
As soon as I set eyes on you.

Julia
You really are so very handsome,
As well as charming and gallant.

Ottavio
I'll be a perfect angel if you wish.

Julia
I think you are a mirror which
Reflects the sun's bright rays, and since
The sun is far away from me, you
Reflect its light, illuminate my life.

Roselo (*aside to* **Julia**)
Because you are between us both,
I am eclipsed by you, but I
shall never be eclipsed by him.
He's so transparent.

Julia

                         So who loves me
The most?

Ottavio

            I do.

Roselo (*whispers*)

                     I do.

Julia
>   To whom do I
>   Belong?

Ottavio
>   To me.

Roselo (*whispers*)
>   To me.

Julia
>   You'll be   300
>   For ever mine?

Ottavio
>   I shall.

Roselo (*whispers*)
>   I shall.

Julia
>   You won't deny it.

Ottavio
>   Never!

Roselo (*whispers*)
>   Never!

Julia
>   You'll meet me, then?

Ottavio
>   Of course!

Roselo (*whispers*)
>   Of course!

Julia
>   A little later?

Ottavio
>   Can't wait.

Roselo (*whispers*)

                Can't wait.

Julia

Who'll be your guide?

Ottavio

                Why, love.

Roselo (*whispers*)

                        Why, love.

Julia

You'll come alone?

Ottavio

              I shall.

Roselo (*whispers*)

                  I shall.

Julia

I'll wait for you?

Ottavio

             Yes, wait.

Roselo (*whispers*)

                 Yes, wait.

Julia

You promise me?

Ottavio

            I do.

Roselo (*whispers*)

            I do.

Julia

Where shall we meet?

Ottavio

              The garden.

Roselo (*whispers*)

The garden.

Julia
Listen!

Ottavio
What is it?

Roselo (*whispers*)
What is it?

Ottavio
The echo of my words. How strange!

Julia
Perhaps you imagined it.

Roselo (*whispers*)
As I
Understand every bit of it.

Julia (*to* **Octavio**)
Don't be alarmed. Whenever we speak of love,
We think our words must echo everywhere,
And others have knowledge of our feelings.

Ottavio
Yes, it must be that.

Antonio
Julia, it's getting late.

Julia
Yes, father. (*To* **Roselo**.) Here, take this!

She gives **Roselo** *a ring.*

Ottavio
Take what?
I can't see anything.

Roselo (*aside*)
Oh, fate
Has favoured me so much!

Julia

Are you confused?   320

Ottavio
Why, yes.

Julia

Well, didn't you see my hand
Was on my heart? That's why I said
'Take this!'

Ottavio

Ah, yes, of course. Your heart.
I'll guard it with my soul.

Roselo (*aside*)

Whoever saw
Such cunning? It's sheer brilliance! She says
'Take this!', gives me the ring, he thinks
She's giving him her heart!

Antonio (*to* **Teobaldo**)

I'm grateful.
You've made me act more sensibly.

Teobaldo
I'm pleased to have been of help.
It's late. Time to end the festivities.

Antonio
Indeed. Servants! Bring some torches!

Teobaldo
God be with you! We'll speak tomorrow.

Dorotea
Goodbye, cousin.

Julia

Goodbye. Take care.

Exit all, except **Julia** *and* **Celia**. **Roselo** *and* **Julia** *exchange looks as he leaves.*

Julia

Celia, wait. I need to speak to you.

Celia

And I to you, my lady. But you
Go first.

Julia

      Tell me, have you ever seen
Such a good-looking boy – the one
Who spoke to me?

Celia

          Do you know who he is?

Julia

I wish I did. I found him so
Attractive that I led him on.   340
I can't believe I was so daring.
I know young men can often put
A spell on girls and make them think
Such thoughts as they should be ashamed of.
He must have done the same to me.
He may have left but, truth to tell,
He's left me totally bewitched.

Celia

          And put
You in a fine pickle! But still,
You shouldn't think he's put a spell
On you. The boy is known to all
The loveliest ladies in Verona.
They all admire his looks and personality.
But, if you fancy him, you ought to know
One thing. Roselo is a Montague.

Julia

I don't believe it! Oh, this is terrible!

Celia

No, don't be sad! It's best you know,
Before it's far too late.

Julia

                It is
Too late. I let him hold my hand.
Oh, God! Who let him in?

Celia

                  I overheard
The older men. They wanted him dead.   360
Let's hope they didn't follow him.

Julia

Oh, go and see! . . . No, stay! . . . I'm just
Confused. And he's alone.

Celia

                He had two friends
With him. And your uncle, Teobaldo, calmed
Things down.

Julia

            I don't know why he came.
He must be mad. If only he'd kept
His mask in place, my father wouldn't have known,
And I wouldn't have fallen in love.

Celia

Be quiet! To say you love him is,
My lady, sheer madness.

Julia

                I wish
I'd never seen him. I respect
My honour.

Celia

          But you've done nothing wrong.
You had your back to him. You were speaking to
Ottavio.

Julia

       That makes it worse.

Celia

But why?

Julia

Because my words were all intended for
Roselo. He understood what I was saying.

Celia

No matter. You did nothing that affects
Your honour.

Julia

I gave him a ring.

Celia

Common enough at these festivities.

Julia

And arranged to meet him in the garden.   380

Celia

Then don't meet him.

Julia

But I'm in love.

Celia

Forget him! Your parents would be furious.

Julia

If only I'd known who he was.
I acted so stupidly. But I found
Him so attractive. If he sees me again,
I don't know what will become of me.
Tomorrow you have to look for him. Tell
Him I know who he is. And tell him too
He must never come here again.

Celia

I shall, my lady. To tell the truth,
I was amazed to hear you speak
To him so freely.

Julia

You should have stopped me.

Celia

I couldn't. I was distracted by his servant.

Julia

Distracted?

Celia

I swear to you. If you
Believe the master is as daring as
He is attractive, so is the servant.

Julia

I need to know more about Roselo.
Find out if someone else attracts him.
My honour is at stake.

Celia

But why?
You told me you'd forget him.

Julia

Yes, so   400
I did. Well, tell him I didn't mean
A word of what I said, that he
Must never come again. But still,
There can't be any harm in knowing if
He loves another.

Celia

That's just as foolish.
You have to let him love whichever girl
He wants. He's not for you!

Julia

Oh, don't
Be so annoying! You always criticise!
You'd try to stop me loving anyone.

Celia

But this is . . .

Julia

              Stop it! Don't be difficult!

Celia

I think it's time for bed.

Julia

                No, I don't want to!

Celia

All right, I promise I'll speak to Roselo.

Julia

Oh, how I love the sound of his name!
Tomorrow you must wear the kind
Of dress Dorotea had on yesterday.

Celia

Who knows? One day Roselo might
Become . . .

Julia

         What?

Celia

            Your husband!

Julia

You said it could never be!

Celia

                They say
That love will always find a way.

Julia

Ah, so now you've changed your mind!   420
Much more agreeable! You see,
The way to keep a lover happy is
To praise his love.

Exit both. Enter **Arnaldo** *and* **Lidio**.

Arnaldo

Lidio, help me remove these spurs.

Lidio

No doubt you've come because you are bored
With village life.

Arnaldo

No, not at all.
I love the countryside. I'm here
Because of family. I'd much
Prefer to be out hunting. Here, take
My gun. Be very careful.

Lidio

You mean
It's loaded?

Arnaldo

So full of shot that if it were
Directed at Antonio Capulet, I'd be
The happiest of men. Tell me,
What news of Roselo?

Lidio

He's very well.

Arnaldo

Studying much?

Lidio

Not that much, no.
But still, he's learning useful things.

Arnaldo

Such as?

Lidio

Fencing, riding, a bit
Of sport.

Arnaldo

You think that 'useful'?

Lidio

                     That's how
The nobles see it, sir, just as they think
That dice and cards are bad.

Arnaldo

                     Is he out   440
At night?

Lidio

                  Can't tell you that. I'm
In bed by ten. His friend, Marín,
Would know.

Arnaldo

                I'm sure he would! And sure too
He doesn't take my boy to midnight mass.
The women he's got chalked up on
His bedpost! None of them virtuous!

Lidio

You'd have to lock him up to put
A stop to that, sir!

Arnaldo

                   If there's a breach
In any castle wall, the place
Becomes an easy target. Such is
My son, a young and inexperienced boy.
Knowing how much he means to me,
My enemies could take his life
And thereby put an end to mine.
A dark night, it's easily done.

Lidio

You ought to get Marín away
From him. He leads him by the nose.

Arnaldo

Maybe. But others would only take
His place. I know these servants!

Lidio

You do, sir?

Arnaldo

                    Well, he's by far the worst   460
Of all. Worse still because he's been
With us so long. When that occurs,
The master often becomes the servant,
And if the servant is aware
Of any failing on his master's part,
Then God forbid!

Lidio

                    But if a servant is
Well bred and sensible, I think
You can rely on him.

Arnaldo

                    Maybe.
In any case, I want my son
To settle down and show more discipline.
I think that marriage could well be
The way to make him act more sensibly.
It makes young men responsible.

Lidio

I'm not so sure, my lord. Not while
Marín advises him. It could
Make matters worse.

Arnaldo

                    In what respect?

Lidio

Well, as you know, while your son
Is young and single, people will
Forgive his indiscretions. But if
He's married and Marín persuades   480
Him to involve himself with dubious women,
It damages both his and your honour.
As well as that, the in-laws will

Be up in arms. You'll have to pay
To cover up his misdemeanours.
His wife will be upset. He'll steal
Her clothes and jewellery to fund
His way of life. He'll not turn up
For meals, stay out all night, become
A never-ending worry to his family.
Imagine all the arguments!
And even worse if he beats up
His wife when she complains about
His love-affairs. Believe me, sir,
It's what will happen in the end.

Arnaldo
You think Marín can cause all that?

Lidio
I do, sir.

Arnaldo
   For you to say these things,
He must have harmed you in some way.

Lidio
I speak the truth. I'm sorry if
You don't believe me.

Arnaldo
     It seems to me   500
That when a servant speaks like this
Of someone else, he has good cause
To either hate or envy him.

Lidio
      That's true
Enough of palaces, my lord.

Arnaldo
      I think
It's true wherever envy reigns.

Lidio

My lord, this isn't fair. The more
I criticise Marín, the more I seem
At fault.

Arnaldo

                    Enough of this! I find
The whole thing tiresome.

Lidio

                                        The truth
Is often tiresome. But don't forget
That loyalty to you obliges me
To tell you what I know.

Exit **Arnaldo**. *Enter* **Marín**.

Marín

Ah, Lidio! What news of grumpy-guts?
I expect he asked about his son.
No doubt a load of cunning questions.

Lidio

As usual.

Marín

                    So did he mention me?
I'm sure he did.

Lidio

                            He mentioned lots
Of things. I told him he shouldn't worry
As long as you were there to guide
And teach Roselo, he needn't have   520
Any sleepless nights. I told him too
The kind of advice you give the boy,
And how you steer him away from all
Temptation.

Marín

                        Oh, what a friend you are!
And what a stroke of luck the day

We met! Remember the wine we shared
And then the girls? Believe me, Lidio, stick
With me, you'll never go without.

Lidio

I'm happy enough with the job I do.

Marín

No, listen. I've met two girls, new to Verona.
I'll introduce you. One of them plays
A lovely guitar.

Lidio

                    I'll go and see
If master's gone to bed. You make
Arrangements.

Marín

                    Whatever you want.

Lidio

In future we'll be the best of friends.

Exit **Lidio**.

Marín

Oh, what a rogue this fellow is!
Dishonesty disguised as piety!
But still, that's what you have to do
If you serve someone else. Your eyes
Wide open, mouth shut tight. You have   540
To learn to crawl, be grateful for
The scraps, tell jokes to keep the bastards all
Amused. In short, you needn't work
Too hard as long as you abuse the rest
And keep the master on your side.
And just one other thing. The truth
Won't get you anywhere.

Enter **Roselo** *and* **Anselmo**.

Roselo

Whoever heard of such bad luck?

Anselmo
>That's who she is. There's nothing you
>Can do.

Roselo
>A girl as beautiful as her
>Turns out to be a Capulet!
>Antonio's daughter! She's made
>A fool of me. What seemed pure honey
>Is merely poison.

Anselmo
>You shouldn't have gone
>To the house.

Roselo
>Ah, Marín!

Marín
>Your father's here.
>Speak quietly.

Roselo
>He'll soon know what
>It is that ails me.

Marín
>Have you gone mad?

Roselo
>Of course I have! Mad about the girl.

Marín
>But she's a Capulet!

Roselo
>It makes
>No difference.

Marín
>Believe me, sir. It's early days,   560
>So you can nip it in the bud.

Anselmo

Take my
Advice. Just forget her! Pretend
You saw her in a picture, or in
A mirror. You turn around, she's gone,
Completely disappeared.

Roselo

Not true!
I may have left the house, but when
I did, I took her image with me.
I have it here, inside, as fresh
As when I first set eyes on her.

Anselmo

My friend, you cannot even think
Of loving her. The whole thing promises
Disaster, for you and for your family.
Just think! One day you venture near
Her house. A Capulet could shoot
You dead.

Roselo

I doubt it.

Anselmo

No, believe it!

Roselo

But you don't understand my feelings.

Anselmo

The only thing I understand
Is that you are their mortal enemy.

Roselo

But she isn't.

Anselmo

What did she say to you?
She's never set eyes on you till now.   580

Roselo

She offered me her hand.

Anselmo

A trick
To lead you on, so they can get
Their hands on you.

Roselo

This ring as well.

Anselmo

It's all too obvious.

Roselo

I've agreed to meet
Her in the garden.

Anselmo

The perfect spot
For you to die.

Roselo

Oh, don't be stupid!
She didn't know me. She loves me,
And I adore her beauty. So don't
Get in my way! I'll speak to her tonight.
I'll go there armed, no matter what
You say. If you, Anselmo, are my friend,
And you, Marín, my servant, both
Of you will come with me.

Anselmo

Oh, very well.
It makes no difference if I die!

Marín

And you know me, sir. The bravest man
You've ever known!

Roselo

The man who loves
As much as this will never find

A greater challenge. But then, my love
Would be less worthy if there were
No obstacles. The day may come,   600
When, through my death, she'll know
How much I loved her.

Exit all. Enter **Julia**, **Ottavio** *and* **Celia**.

Ottavio
I don't understand you.

Julia
                    Nor I you.

Ottavio
But you told me to come.

Julia
                    I did?

Ottavio
Of course you did! If not, why are you here?

Julia
Perhaps to get annoyed if you dared
To come.

Ottavio
                    You told me at the party
To meet you tonight.

Julia
                    Ottavio, my father's still
Awake. Go and keep him company.
Amuse him, get him to go to bed,
And then come down. You'll see for yourself
What my feelings are.

Ottavio
                    You promise?

Julia
I promise.

Ottavio

I'll make quite sure that, after dinner,
He doesn't join the family.

Julia

I'll still
Be here.

Ottavio

Oh, heavens, send sweet oblivion on
This house. Let sleep envelop it.

Exit **Ottavio**.

Julia

Celia . . .

Celia

My lady . . .

Julia

What shall I do?

Celia

I think that, if Roselo comes,
You ought to disillusion him.

Julia

You think so?

Celia

Yes.

Julia

Denying love   620
Would be so cruel!

Celia (*aside*)

Oh, this girl
Is so naive! She uses a lover
So she can entertain another.
(*Aloud.*) I see you've sent Ottavio off
To speak with your father.

Julia

Well, better that
Than have him stop me speaking to
Roselo.

Celia

Listen! What's that?

Julia

Roselo!
I know it's him!

Celia

He must have climbed
The garden wall.

Julia

I pray to God
He doesn't fall. Roselo!

Enter **Roselo**, *handsomely dressed.*

Roselo

My lady, may
I speak to you?

Julia

You may, provided that
You show the modesty appropriate
To me, as well as to yourself.
But first, before you flatter me
With pleasing words, as men so often do,
You have to know I know exactly who
You are. It grieves me that you are
Who you are, and also that I'm who I am.
What could be worse – me a Capulet
And you a Montague? When I   640
Set eyes on you, I found you most
Attractive – as other women say
They do throughout Verona.
Because of that, I told you you
Could meet me here, believing that,

If we were equals, you might wish
To be my suitor. But then I heard
Your name and all the joy I felt
Gave way to fear, for you as well
As for myself. So now I ask
One thing: not that you return
The ring, nor that you ever say
I didn't love you. All I ask
Is that you do not speak, and that
You leave the way you came. I don't
Want any harm to come to you.
Just leave.

Roselo
          What can I say? I'd do
It if I could, but now it isn't possible.
It's easy enough to give you the ring.
It's easy to forget I climbed the wall   660
And spoke to you. But not to see
Or speak to you again because
It's dangerous, what sign is that
Of love? I do admit, when I set eyes
On you and fell in love, I didn't know
Your name. But when I did, and realised
The danger I was in, like you I thought
It best we never meet again.
But love cannot be set aside.
It overcomes all obstacles, and so,
Sweet Julia, tells me I shouldn't
Stop loving you. My dearest, sweetest Julia,
Love favours us and . . .

Julia
             No, stop! And please
Stop calling me 'sweet Julia'. It makes
Me feel the way I shouldn't feel.
In any case, how can you see
Or speak to me? There's nothing we
Can do.

Roselo

> We could get married, secretly.
> I have a friend. He could arrange
> It, marry us.

Julia

> It frightens me.

Roselo

> But why?   680

Julia

> It's far too dangerous.

Roselo

> But don't you see?
> If we were married, that could put
> An end to all the enmity between
> Our families. It could well be
> That this is what heaven wants, so everyone
> Can live in peace through our good
> And honest love.

Julia

> Please, say no more.
> You'd better go before my cousin comes.
> I don't know why I fell in love with you.

Roselo

> So what's your answer?

Julia

> I'll meet you at
> The parish church. Bring the friend
> You say can marry us. I've listened to
> Your words and failed to block my ears,
> So now I shall be blind, like love itself.
> Go quickly, someone's coming.

Roselo

> You
> Should leave as well. Avoid your cousin.

Julia

Promise you won't forget me!

Roselo

In God's name!

You think I would?

Julia

Don't take God's name

In vain!

Roselo

So what should I say?

Julia

Only that

You love me.

Celia

My lady! Footsteps!   700

Roselo

Give me your hand!

Julia

Embrace me!

Marín (*off*)

Quickly!

Julia

Go!

Act Two

Enter **Teobaldo** *and* **Fesenio**.

Teobaldo
Is Dorotea still inside the church?

Fesenio
She is. And full of sadness and anxiety.
Two Montagues – Dorina and
Andrea – seized her private chair.

Teobaldo
Were there no Capulets to put
A stop to it?

Fesenio
                    I doubt the bravest would
Have been of any use. You can't
Have fighting in a church. The Capulets
Were happy to discuss the matter,
But then a crowd of Montagues appeared
And so the Capulets backed down.

Teobaldo
Backed down? What do you mean?

Fesenio
They didn't make a fuss.

Teobaldo
                    That's what
I'm asking. They behaved like cowards.
You say she's still inside the church?

Fesenio
Indeed, but saying nothing. She's more
Concerned with your peace of mind.

Teobaldo
By God, are female Capulets
Less worthy than the Montagues?

Fesenio

You shouldn't think like that. No need   20
To be upset.

Teobaldo

                No doubt they threw
The cushions as far from the chair
As possible!

Fesenio

                If you believe yourself
To be, like all your family, a man
Of peace, why get so angry over this?
You wouldn't want to be the cause
Of further arguments between
The families. Who knows where it
Might lead?

Teobaldo

                So must I suffer this
And not complain?

Fesenio

                        It could be worse.

Teobaldo

It's bad enough. Seizing a lady's chair
And she of noble birth and lineage!

Enter **Ottavio**, *accompanying* **Julia**; **Celia** *and servants.*

Julia

So Dorotea's here already?

Ottavio

She came ahead of us, an hour ago.

Julia

But why so early?

Ottavio

                She thought you'd be
Here too, that you were keen to hear

The priest, such is his reputation.

Julia

You should have mentioned it last night.
My mother's so devout she would
Have had us here at crack of dawn.   40

Ottavio

I'm afraid the church is almost full.

Exit **Julia**, **Ottavio**, **Celia** *and servants.*

Teobaldo

Is that my son?

Fesenio

Why, yes. He's with
His cousin, Julia. He's obviously very fond
Of her. They've gone inside.

Teobaldo

Tell him
I want to speak to him.

Fesenio

I'll fetch
Him for you.

Exit **Fesenio**.

Teobaldo

This is an insult to
Our family name! Oh, I detest
These people! Throughout my life
I've recommended peace and harmony,
But nothing like this had happened to me then.
It makes my blood boil!

Enter **Ottavio** *and* **Fesenio**.

Ottavio

You wish to see
Me, father?

Teobaldo

    I do indeed! How can
You be indifferent to the things
I value most? You spend your time
Attempting to impress your cousin,
And showing no concern for your sister.
You'd rather chase a dream that is
Impossible than pay attention to
The honour of our family!

Ottavio

But why are you so angry? Tell me!   60

Teobaldo

I promise you, I have good cause.
If you'd gone with your sister and been
There when she needed help, I'd have
No cause to lose my temper, nor
To feel ashamed.

Ottavio

    Ashamed of what?
What's happened?

Teobaldo

    If only I were young
And had your strength, I'd show these people.
As you can guess, it has to do
With our family's good name.

Ottavio

So who's offended you?

Teobaldo

    No, wait
Until you've heard it all.

Ottavio

    Oh, yes, and have
You call me coward too! Who is
It? Tell me!

Teobaldo

Your sister's private chair.
They've taken it and doubtless ruined it.

Ottavio

But who?

Teobaldo

Inside. You'll soon find out.

Ottavio

Then you wait here.

Teobaldo

No, I'll come with you.

Ottavio

It might not be safe.

Teobaldo

I have to do it.

Exit **Teobaldo** *and* **Ottavio**.

Fesenio

He's pushed him into it and now
He's gone with him. What stupidity!

Enter **Roselo** *and* **Anselmo**.

Roselo

I saw her with Ottavio.

Anselmo

I thought   80
That you'd forgotten her. While I've
Been gone, you haven't mentioned her.

Roselo

In case you might be shocked. But more
Than that, I couldn't put my secret in
A letter.

Fesenio (*aside*)

The Montagues! This could

Get out of hand. I'll find Ottavio, see
What he intends to do.

He enters the church.

Anselmo

What secret, then?

Roselo

I need to tell you all that's happened since
You've been away. You won't believe it.

Anselmo

All right. I'm listening.

Roselo

The night you came
With me and helped me climb the garden wall
So I could speak with her, Julia and I
Agreed to marry, secretly, in church.
I managed to persuade the priest, Aurelio,
Despite his doubts. He saw how desperate
I was. So Julia came with Celia, letting it
Be known she wanted to confess
In one of the chapels. Her servants left,
Aurelio and I arrived, and, since
He knew what our intentions were,   100
He married us.

Anselmo

You must be mad!

Roselo

Why mad? He knew, if he refused
To marry us, it would have been
Disastrous. Imagine what would happen
If we were meeting secretly
And someone got to know of it.
Our families would soon be at
Each other's throats. And so he thought
It best that we be married.

Anselmo
Why not
Say 'dead'? When this is known, the end
Will be the same.

Roselo
Perhaps heaven will
Protect us.

Anselmo
You cannot hide your feelings.
You walk along her street and see
Her at the window, or here in church.

Roselo
I shall be careful.

Anselmo
Is any man in love
That careful?

Roselo
I avoid her street.
I only go to church for mass.

Anselmo
So how do you see each other?

Roselo
It's quite safe, Anselmo.

Anselmo
Tell me!

Roselo
I climb the garden wall at night.   120
The cedars and the orange trees
Protect me. Then Celia takes me
To Julia's room. Before it's light,
I climb back down the garden wall
And spend the day at home, catching up
On sleep.

Anselmo

You call that being careful?

Roselo

It's safe enough. All Verona's fast
Asleep.

Anselmo

I guarantee Ottavio's not.

Roselo

He loves her, I know. But Julia's clever.

Anselmo

How
Exactly?

Roselo

She meets him in the garden, talks
To him from ten till twelve. And then
He leaves quite happily.

Anselmo

It's neat
Enough. But aren't you jealous that
He meets your wife?

Roselo

Why should I be?
I often watch and listen, hidden in
The trees. Their conversation is
Quite innocent.

Anselmo

And your relationship
With her?

Roselo

A husband's with his wife.

Anselmo

You mean the marriage has been consummated?

Roselo
What do you expect?

Anselmo
It makes me so   140
Afraid.

Roselo
It doesn't me.

Anselmo
You ought to be
Afraid of them.

Roselo
I fear nothing.
My love for her fills me with courage.

Anselmo
I don't know what to say.

Roselo
Then best
Say nothing. To offer me advice
Would be like spitting in the wind.

Anselmo
So what do you propose to do?

Roselo
I'll just be patient, and wait for time
To overcome these obstacles.

Arnaldo, **Antonio** *and* **Teobaldo** *offstage.*

Antonio (*off*)
Get out of here, you cowards!

Arnaldo (*off*)
Get out
Yourselves, you Capulets! Cowards, all
Of you!

Sounds of a sword-fight off.

Roselo

What's going on?

Teobaldo (*off*)

You aren't
As brave as you think you are.

Antonio (*off*)

Give us
The cushions, or we'll send you to hell!

Arnaldo (*off*)
I don't know what you mean.

Antonio (*off*)

Get out
Of here.

Roselo

My father's voice!

Anselmo

Roselo, wait!

Roselo
I can't. Let's see what's going on!

Roselo *enters the church.*

Anselmo
My God!

They exit the church with swords drawn: **Antonio**, **Teobaldo**,
Ottavio, *and* **Fesenio** *to one side; to the other,* **Arnaldo**,
Lidio, **Marín**, *and* **Anselmo**. **Roselo** *stands between them,
centre stage.*

Roselo

Anselmo, stay close to my father!
(*Aside* to **Anselmo**.) Although my blood incites me to
The opposite, Julia makes me calm   160
Things down.

Anselmo

What can I say? (*Aside.*) Love blinds
Him utterly.

Roselo

Gentlemen, hold fast!
Although I am a Montague,
I have no wish to cause you harm.
What's caused this argument? Is there
No reason why it can't be solved
With common sense? Why, all of you
Are brave and honest noblemen.
Is this so serious that we cannot find
A resolution?

Ottavio

We've been insulted.

Roselo

But how? Tell me, Ottavio.

Ottavio (*to the others*)

They have
To die!

Roselo

Explain, Ottavio! Don't
Be so impetuous.

Ottavio

We ought
To have the old men leave and settle this
Between the two of us.

Roselo

My father stays.
I always turn to him for good
Advice. Now as for this dispute,
Remember I want to be your friend,
Even if you aren't so fond of me.

Ottavio

                                   Keep
Your friendship!

Roselo

                   But why?

Ottavio

                          You're nothing but   180
A coward!

Roselo

          Ottavio, this does
Your reputation little credit. Choose
Your words more carefully!

Ottavio

                        So is it right
That when my sister's servant brings
Her private chair to church, yours should
Remove it?

Roselo

          Of course not, no, and we
Shall make it up to you.

Arnaldo

                  The servant wasn't one
Of ours.

Teobaldo

          Whose was he, then?

Arnaldo

                 Andrea's.

Roselo

Ottavio, all I want is that we live
In peace. So let's go in. I'll place
Your sister's chair where it has pride
Of place.

Ottavio
                    That would improve things.
But nothing can excuse the insults.

Roselo
If that was unacceptable, I have
The answer. You marry Andrea,
I marry Julia. What do you say?

Ottavio
I'd rather kill myself than witness it.

Roselo
That would at least avoid your death
At someone else's hands.

Ottavio
                    You dare
To speak to me like that? I'll kill   200
You, you effeminate creature!

Roselo
                    Listen to
Me, wait!

Ottavio
          Why wait? Come, draw your sword!

Roselo
My friends, you see how he's provoking me
When all I want is that we live
In peace.

Ottavio
          Come on, don't be such a coward!

Roselo (*aside*)
Forgive me, Julia! If I held back, you
Were the reason why, not cowardice.

They draw swords. **Ottavio** *falls.*

Teobaldo
He's killed my son!

Roselo

               Father, this way!

Let's go!

Exit **Roselo**, **Arnaldo**, **Anselmo**, **Lidio**, *and* **Marín**.

Antonio

      Capulets! Here quickly!

Ottavio

      I must confess my sins.

Teobaldo

               My son

Is dying.

Antonio

          Get him inside! Attend

To his soul!

Teobaldo

         I am to blame for this!

Ottavio *is carried into the church. The onlookers disperse.*

Fesenio

      Teobaldo led a quiet life,

But now he is in torment. The mistake

Was his, and since he was to blame,

He should forgive Roselo. He had

To defend himself, as well as his

Good name.

Enter the **Duke of Verona**, *a* **Captain**, *soldiers.*

Verona

          Whoever is responsible

Shall die.

Captain

         It seems the man to blame

Is Teobaldo Capulet.   220

Verona
Were many hurt?

Captain
                    On both sides?

Verona
                            Dead?

Captain
Ottavio, Teobaldo's son.

Verona
                    Where is
The body?

Captain
            Inside the church. Before
He died, they gave him absolution,
In the presence of his father and his sisters.

Verona
So who killed him?

Captain
                    Roselo Montague,
Arnaldo's son. But everyone
Agrees he was provoked and that
The crime was much more self-defence
Than murder.

Verona
                    Aren't you a Montague,
Some sort of relative?

Captain
                            By no means, sir.
And nor am I a Capulet.
I favour neither family.

Fesenio
My lord, I'm Teobaldo's servant.
I loved Ottavio like a brother.

I grew up in the house, but even so,
I have to say Ottavio was to blame.
He was, to say the least, provocative,
His insults unacceptable.
Roselo asked the onlookers   240
To be his witnesses, to swear
That what he did was self-defence.

Captain
You see, my lord, the case is clear
Enough.

Fesenio
            You only have to question those
Who saw it.

Verona
            Where is Roselo now?

Captain
He's taken refuge in the tower there,
My lord, defended by a servant.

Verona
Roselo! Listen!

Roselo *and* **Marín** *appear at the window of the tower, the latter holding a fistful of stones.*

Roselo
            Who is it?

Captain
                        You ought
To recognise the Duke, my friend.

Roselo
My lord, what do you want of me?

Verona
I want you to come down. I guarantee
Your safety.

Roselo

> I shall if you protect
> Me from my enemies. I'll place
> My sword at your feet. Unless
> You promise this, I'll stay and fight.
> I'd rather starve to death than die
> A prisoner of the Capulets.

Verona

> I give you my word.

Roselo

> Then I accept.

Marín

> Be very careful, master!

Roselo

> The man
> Who's innocent should fear nothing.   260

*Exit **Roselo**, the **Duke**, the **Captain**, soldiers.*

Marín

> Far better if we'd got away
> From here and not involved ourselves
> With bleeding lawyers and with witnesses.
> God knows, some rogue will swear he saw
> It all when he was nowhere near the scene.
> And someone else will make a statement as
> It takes his fancy. I doubt that any good
> Will come of it.

*Exit **Marín**. Enter **Julia** and **Celia**.*

Julia

> I've nothing to fear, nothing to lose
> As far as honour is concerned.

Celia

> Madam, your husband there!

Julia

What's this?
Have they arrested him?

Enter the **Captain**.

Captain

Stop! Who are you?

Julia
I'm Julia Capulet.

Captain

Ah, yes,
Antonio's daughter.

Enter **Roselo** *and* **Marín**, *guarded by soldiers.*

Soldier

Roselo Montague, sir!

Roselo (*aside to* **Marín**)
Marín, it's Julia!

Marín

She's here to blame
You for her cousin's death.

Enter the **Duke of Verona**.

Verona
Roselo Montague, you killed
Ottavio Capulet, did you not?

Roselo
I did, but under provocation.
It was a case of self-defence.   280

Verona
This lady is Ottavio's cousin. She
Was close to him.

Roselo
Then she can tell
Us if his death was justified.

Julia

    Ottavio was my cousin and my friend.
    But even so, although I do
    No favours to my family,
    I have to tell the truth. He was to blame.

Verona

    You saw the incident?

Julia

              I did.
    And others will agree with me.
    Roselo tried to calm him down.
    Ottavio, though, has always been
    Pig-headed. He lost his temper.
    (*Aside to* **Celia**.) May God forgive me! I saw nothing.

Verona

    What does your servant say?

Celia

              I know
    Ottavio went to look for him.
    As well as hating him, the man
    Was jealous of Roselo. He had
    A group of friends with him, and when
    He saw Roselo, he drew his sword.
    (*Aside to* **Julia**.) May God forgive me too, my lady!   300

Captain

    The people in the church will say
    The same, my lord.

Julia

             No one will speak
    Against Roselo.

Verona

            In that case, what
    Am I to do, Captain?

Captain
                    He should
Be exiled from Verona. If not,
There could be serious trouble and your
Authority might well be undermined.
Undoubtedly, he's innocent
Of murder, but this is still a serious matter.

Verona
It seems a fair solution.

Captain
                    I think
You need to issue a command,
Instructing everyone to keep
The peace or risk arrest and death.

Verona
It shall be done. I'll sign the order.

Captain
And in the meantime Roselo should
Have some protection.

Roselo
                    Captain, there's
No need. I can defend myself.

Verona
It's for the best while tempers still
Run high. Good lady, may God be with you!
Roselo comes with me.

Julia (*aside*)
                    Oh, this   320
Is more than I can bear!

Verona
                    You'll stay
At my palace until you leave.

Roselo
Just as you wish, my lord.

Julia (*aside*)
                    Celia,
Let's go, before my disappointment makes
Things worse.

Celia
                    Today has proved it never rains
Unless it pours.

Roselo (*aside*)
                    My poor, dearest Julia!

Julia (*aside*)
Roselo, my one and only love!

Exit all. Enter **Teobaldo** *and* **Dorotea**.

Teobaldo
The fault was mine entirely!
There's no one else to blame.

Dorotea
                              Let's hope
That justice will be done.

Teobaldo
                    To have
To live with this! Though honour is
Above all family ties, what kind
Of father drives his son to take
Revenge, only to bring about
His death?

Dorotea
              But everyone blames Ottavio.
Roselo tried to calm him down
But failed. It only made things worse . . .
But what's the point? What's done is done.

Teobaldo
I don't deserve to go on living.
My son will soon be buried in   340
The family grave, his youthful looks

Concealed beneath a slab of cold,
Unfeeling marble. Meanwhile, the Montague
Responsible for this escapes,
Finds refuge in another land.
It cannot be! We have to seek
Revenge. All members of our family
Must know of this.

Fesenio

               They failed to find
Him, sir. I've heard he's being sent
To Rome. The Duke's guards go with
Him until they reach Ferrara. They think
All this will pacify the Capulets,
And satisfy all those who blame
Ottavio for his insolence . . .

Teobaldo

Enough! You think I'm made of stone?
This grief is more than I can bear,
And still they say that I'm to blame.
Such cowards, all of them, so quick
To make their accusations. But I
Shall take revenge, I swear. The Duke   360
Shall hear of this. I've lost my son.
Why should his murderer live on?

Exit **Teobaldo**.

Dorotea

Look what you've done to him!

Fesenio

               I spoke
The truth, my lady. I know I'm but
A servant, but that doesn't mean
I shouldn't tell the truth. The fact
Is everyone now blames your brother.

Dorotea

I know. But though I'll miss him, I pray

That heaven sees fit to spare Roselo.

Fesenio
But how can you say that?

Dorotea
                                He's much
Admired by the ladies in Verona,
And praised by all the Capulets
For courage, looks and personality.
I know as well that Julia fancied him.

Fesenio
The drums! The Duke's decision!

Dorotea
See what it says.

Exit both. Enter **Roselo** *and* **Marín**, *both dressed as travellers.*

Roselo
Have you got the ladder?

Marín
                                Of course!
I've set it up, sir. Much better
To be prepared, should someone take
Us by surprise.

Roselo
                    You fancy Celia.   380
That's why you moved so fast.

Marín
                                I did it
For both of us.

Roselo
                    So are you seeing her,
As I am Julia?

Marín
                    I wouldn't have come
On Celia's account alone. It's just

That everything has come together.
You know, sir, your cheek amazes me.
You got inside and no one saw you!

Roselo
More luck than judgement. But now
My luck's run out.

Marín
                        Hear that?

Roselo
                                    Get ready to
Defend yourself!

Marín
                        Maybe it's just
The sound of water.

Enter **Julia** *and* **Celia**.

Julia
                        Roselo, is that you?

Roselo
Julia, I'm here! God give me patience!
My life is meaningless if what
Inspires it is lost. Julia, I am
Your husband at all times, for good
Or ill, when present and when absent.
I know you'll weep when I am gone,
But dry your tears now before
Your sobs are overheard and I
Am seen. But if you want a sword   400
To put an end to our misfortunes, I'm quite
Prepared for it. Our lives may well
Be sacrificed, but those who want
Me dead can never separate our souls.
You know that I am not to blame
For your cousin's death. To say
I am would be to go against
What others saw to be the truth.

For your sake I thought it best
To suffer all Ottavio's gibes.
But if his life means more to you
Than mine, then take this dagger, use
It on me now and quell your anger with
My death.

Marín

My dearest Celia, you might
With reason think me cowardly
Because I couldn't bear to watch
The fight and claimed it went against
The teachings of the Church. If so,
I offer you my dagger. It's best
You stab yourself and so avoid   420
Arrest for stabbing me.

Julia

Roselo, if
I've risked so many things, why should
A cousin mean much more to me
Than you? If you demanded that
I spill the blood of all my family,
I would, and then I'd offer you
My own. You are my guardian, my
Protection, my only remedy.
In body I'm a Capulet,
A Montague in soul and spirit.

Celia

Marín, my dearest beloved,
Why do you think I'd want you to
Be brave? Why, if you were, they might
Have killed you in that fight, and you'd
Be lost to me. You couldn't give
Me pleasure any more. In my view, brave
Men die and cowards go on living.
A brave man boasts, attracts the police,
And causes trouble in the streets.
That's why you have to be a coward.   440

Why, lily-livered men enjoy
Themselves, dress up in all their finery,
While brave men get caught up in fights,
Can't take things easy, and can't
Resist whatever trouble comes along.
And by the way, as far as stabbing you's
Concerned, I can't, so here's the cellar keys.
Go spill some wine, pretend it's your blood.
You are my life, my refuge, my protection.
In body I am Celia, but in spirit, my
Marín, I am Marina!

Roselo

               So tell
Me, Julia, what are we to do?

Julia

We go on meeting secretly
At night, as often as you can,
Scaling the walls, until the moment comes
When we can both escape to Venice.
I shan't be happy until we are
Together. Promise me we shall be!

Roselo

Of course I do! How can you doubt
My love? I'd rather see our families   460
At war, myself the victim of
My enemies, than break my promise.

Celia

So will you meet me too, Marín?

Marín

I promise I'll do everything
I can, provided I don't come
To any harm, and that the inns
Along the way have food and wine
Enough to keep me going. But what
About you, my sweet? Will you be faithful?

Celia
  As firm and steady as a rock,
  Or maybe a cloud, or thistledown.
  As long as I enjoy your love.

Antonio (*off*)
  Lucio, the gun. There's someone out there.

Julia
  It's father!

Roselo (*to* **Marín**)
          The ladder!

Marín
                Let's go!

Celia
                      No, wait!

Marín
  There isn't time!

Julia
                Are your friends outside?

Roselo
  Anselmo and six others.

Julia
                Take care!

Roselo (*to* **Marín**)
  Come on! No need to be so scared!

Exit both. Enter **Antonio** *and* **Lucio**.

Celia
  What are you going to say?

Lucio
                Look, there!

Antonio
  Go on, then. Fire!

Julia

No, wait!

Antonio

Is that

You, Julia?

Julia

Yes.

Antonio

So who's that with you?   480

Julia

It's Celia.

Antonio

Why are you here? It's late.

Julia

I couldn't sleep, for thinking of
Ottavio. I came outside so no one else
Would hear me crying.

Antonio

I doubt that that

Will bring him back.

Julia

I know it won't,
But even the hardest stone would grieve
For him. As for myself, I've lost
A husband!

Antonio

I don't know what you mean!

Julia

He would have been my husband.
So why are you surprised that I
Now weep on that account?
Believe me, father, women are
Much gentler than men. They feel

And weep, and justly so, while men
Are hard as stone, feel nothing, kill,
Wage war, or take revenge. I pray to God
That this does not rebound on our family!

Exit **Julia** *and* **Celia**.

Lucio

She's most upset.

Antonio

              She is indeed.

Lucio

And no surprise if, as she says,
Your squabbles with the Montagues   500
Have robbed her of a husband.

Antonio

I must admit, I hadn't thought
Of him in quite that way. But still,
As long as I'm alive, I shall
Protect her interests. If only I'd known
She loved Ottavio, this would not
Have happened. Why, more than once
My brother said they should be married.
But I did nothing, thinking that
She didn't care for him. I told him so.
But now Ottavio's dead and she,
Quite clearly, grieves for him, I feel
It even more. I cherish the girl.
I think it might be best if I do all
I can to find a rich and eligible man
To marry her. Before he left,
The Count of Paris asked me for
Her hand. And now, I'm told, he's back.
What do you think? A better catch
Than poor Ottavio?

Lucio

              No comparison.   520

The Count's a gentleman, and rich
At that. You ought to speak to her,
See how she feels.

Antonio

A suitor's death
Is, for the girl he's left behind,
Just like the setting sun. The world
Grows dark. But when another sun
Appears the following day, the sadness of
The past is soon forgotten.

Exit both. Enter the **Count of Paris**, **Roselo**, **Marín** *and*
servants.

Paris

I can't think why our meeting should
Upset you in the least. I'm not
Your enemy; it's quite the opposite.
Why, who could say of me I sided with
The Capulets?

Roselo

You must excuse
Me, sir. My mood is dark and so
Distorts the meaning of my words.
My state of mind is such, emotion clouds
My reason. I cannot say if I'm
Alive or dead. I run away
From all that I desire most,
And act in such a cowardly way,   540
I seem more like a Capulet
Than all the Capulets who now
Pursue me.

Paris

Roselo, if I've
Protected you at such a dangerous time,
It's more than just. I'm happy to
Have done so. I wouldn't want a man
As worthy as yourself to be

The victim of an act of treachery.
And even though Ottavio was
A friend of mine, I know he acted rashly,
And you were not to blame. You know,
I'd hoped to marry Julia, and so,
To some extent, I thought myself
A Capulet. Her father, though,
Delayed so long in giving me
Her hand, that now I've lost all interest.
No longer do I feel myself
To be a Capulet. I'm more
Inclined towards the Montagues,
And so, if you agree, I'll ride   560
With you until we reach Ferrara.
I know that you'll be safe with me.

Roselo

I'm grateful, sir. In helping me
You've shown nobility of spirit.
I'll be for ever in your debt
For saving me from such an ambush.
But now I feel quite safe. Ferrara's close
At hand. Verona needs you. You should
Return and pacify its people.
In future I shall see you as
A Montague and let my people know
How you helped to save my life.

Enter **Fesenio**.

Paris

Someone's there.

Roselo

                    Who are you?

Fesenio

                                        Who
Are you?

Paris
> The Count of Paris.

Fesenio
> > This letter is
> For you, my lord.

Paris
> > Roselo, have
> No fear. You are quite safe. So who's
> The letter from?

Fesenio
> > Antonio Capulet.

Marín (*aside to* **Roselo**)
> So shall I shoot him?

Roselo (*to* **Marín**)
> > No, let him go
> In peace.

Marín
> > What if the letter tells
> The Count to kill you?

Roselo
> > A happy end   580
> For anyone as sad as I.

Marín
> > See how
> He studies what it says.

Roselo
> > Perhaps
> It does demand my death.

Marín
> > Then take
> No prisoners! Just run him through!

Roselo
> How can I when he saved my life?

Marín

> This is no time for honour's niceties,
> Nor is it treachery to save
> Your skin. Besides, the man who dies
> Because he cherished niceties,
> Might, when he's dead, be seen as cowardly.

Paris (*to* **Roselo**)

> Roselo, read the letter. It's only right
> You share my happiness. And even if
> I am to be the son-in-law
> Of your most hated enemy,
> That doesn't mean I'll cease to be
> Your friend.

Roselo

> > I don't know what you mean.

Paris

> Then read the letter.

Roselo (*reads aloud*)

> > 'If anything
> Can ease my pain, I do believe
> That that would be your presence in
> My house. I know you favour us,   600
> The Capulets, and love Verona too.
> Roselo, as you will have heard,
> Has killed my nephew. All of us
> Seek justice in his name. We ask
> That you protect us, and I that you
> Become my son-in-law. Julia waits
> For you . . . ' (*Aside.*) I don't believe it!

Paris

> What is it?

Roselo

> > If Julia is to be your wife,
> It puts my life at risk. What more
> Is there to say? You are a Capulet.

You are obliged to kill me.

Paris

                         Of course
I'm not! No matter what you think,
I'm not the kind of person who,
Because of this, would not respect
You as a friend. I came across
You when you needed help, before
I knew the contents of this letter,
And so I felt obliged to help you out.
But now that Julia is to be
My wife, I cannot help you any more,   620
Despite our friendship. It goes against
The kind of man I am, but there
It is. And since you shan't be in
Verona, where I intend to live
With her, there'll be no problem. As for
Fesenio, he's not to say I helped you or
Allowed you to escape.

Fesenio

                       I promise, sir.
I serve the Capulets but, more than that,
I like Roselo.

Paris

               We'll say goodbye, then.

Fesenio
Marín!

Paris (*aside to* **Fesenio**)
            Roselo's so afraid,
He doesn't answer. The very thought
Of death makes great men seem like pygmies.

Exit **Paris**, **Fesenio**, *and servants.*

Marín
You see the danger that we're in.
We could be killed a thousand times

Before we reach Ferrara. You have
To set aside these dreams of love.
Let Julia marry! Let her make
Her bed and lie on it!

Roselo

Julia marry?

Marín

All right, sir. Keep your voice down!

Roselo

Who would have thought that such an angel   640
Could be so fickle? But then, it's said
That angels move with such great speed
That in a single day they fly
From pole to pole. And that is what
She's done: flown off with such velocity
That in a flash my world has been
Transformed from heaven to hell.
Oh, what a fool I was! Those eyes
In which I thought I saw true love
Have flattered only to deceive,
And what was joy are tears to drown
This blaze that turns my heart to ash.
I know that no one loves you as
I do or ever will. On your part,
Such flawless beauty; on mine as well,
If not enough to rival yours. The two
Of us a perfect match. And yet
You choose a man who neither knows
Nor loves you as I do. Your father thinks
That such a marriage brings great honour to   660
His family, and fears me because I killed
Ottavio. As for yourself, perhaps
You think you'll be a greater lady than
You are. But you will not!

Marín

Be quiet!

Roselo
>   Why? Can't I say my piece? It's full moon,
>   When men go mad.

Marín
>   At least you're honest!

Roselo
>   You'd be a noble lady if you were
>   With me! What are great titles but
>   A relic of the past, nobility
>   Inherited from wars long gone?
>   I may not have a family crest
>   Adorned with gold, but still I know
>   I am a man of worth. My hope
>   Is that you'll see the error of
>   Your ways and change your mind. It's not
>   That I am arrogant, but happiness
>   Will not be found in wealth and power, only in
>   Those things in which the spirit takes
>   Delight. A prince's throne may please
>   By day, but will that prince be quite   680
>   As pleasing when he shares your bed
>   At night? I cannot bear the thought
>   Of it. It burns my soul that she
>   Who loved me yesterday should so
>   Betray me now! But what's the point?
>   Why waste my energy on such self-pity?
>   I have to be more dignified
>   And not indulge myself in such abuse!

Marín
>   And quite right too! Why waste your time
>   In getting back at anyone
>   With words?

Roselo
>   So what do you suggest? Deeds
>   Instead?

Marín

Why not?

Roselo

But how?

Marín

Get married in
Ferrara.

Roselo

I see.

Marín

Let's go!

Roselo

They say
That all is fair in love and war.
She's made me suffer. She shall suffer too.

Act Three

Enter **Antonio** *and* **Julia**.

Antonio
You'll do exactly as I say,
Or else!

Julia
                Father, I cannot.

Antonio
                                It's my
Decision that you marry!

Julia
                                The Count
Had every opportunity to kill
Roselo. He failed to take it, and so
He's failed me too.

Antonio
                        I think the heavens
Protect the boy. He seems immune
To every danger.

Julia
                        He shouldn't have
Escaped the Count.

Antonio
                        So are you saying
You cannot marry him because
He failed to avenge Ottavio's death?
You must have loved him more than I
Imagined.

Julia
                I hid my grief as best
I could for many days, but I'm
Not strong enough to go on hiding it.

Antonio

    I understand you need redress,
But that would clearly be possible
If you were married to the Count.
Why, knowing that you want Roselo dead,
He'll leave no stone unturned. You have   20
To marry him. I've given him
My word. He's on his way here.

Julia

                           But it's

Impossible!

Antonio

           If only I'd known,
I'd not have said a word to him.
But now it's done. It's far too late
To change my mind. As far as I'm
Concerned, you are his wife already.

Julia

    Please, father!

Antonio

              Julia, understand
I've no desire to be harsh.
It wasn't I who caused Ottavio's death.
As for this marriage, I gave my word.
To break it now does not become
A man of honour.

Julia (*aside*)

              What could be worse
Than this? I'm so afraid! There's no escape.

Antonio

    So what am I to tell the Count?

Julia

    Best tell him that I'll marry him.
My mind's made up.

Antonio

Are you quite sure?

Julia

What else is to be done? I have
No wish to disobey my father,
And more so when it has to do   40
With honour. The Count shall be my husband.

Antonio

My dear Julia! I am the happiest
Of men, and you the most considerate
Of daughters! As your reward – and this
Apart from what your mother left
And I intend to give you later –
Accept these diamonds, and for
Your husband six thousand ducats.

Julia (*aside*)

This is the death of me!

Antonio

The wedding shall
Take place tonight. Arrangements must
Be made immediately.

Julia (*aside*)

No poison can
Be deadlier than what I feel
Inside!

Antonio

Fesenio, inform the Capulets!
The honour of our family's restored.

Exit **Antonio**.

Julia

How many women in the past
Have killed themselves for love? Dido, queen
Of Carthage; Lucretia, and many more.
As for myself, there is no fire,

Or rope, or knife, or sword, can equal all
This pain!

Enter **Celia**.

Celia

        Madam, I've spoken with   60
Aurelio. I gave him your note.

Julia

So did he read it?

Celia

        It made him weep.
And then he spent an hour in
His room. Afterwards he gave me this –
For you to drink.

Julia

        Are you quite sure?

Celia

Oh, yes.

Julia

        It's true I told him that
I'd rather die than marry. He knows
I love Roselo. That's why he sends
Me this.

Celia

        He is extremely wise, madam.

Julia

And very fond of both Roselo and
Myself. He treats us as his own.
He is the only one who knows
The truth about our marriage. They say
That he's an expert when it comes
To drugs and potions, so all I hope
Is that this isn't something which
Will make me love the Count and then
Forget Roselo.

Celia
I'm sure it isn't.
He knows about your marriage and wants
To avoid a second one. That's why   80
He's given you the potion. He sees
It as the only remedy.

Julia
And so
It shall be. My death shall end this pain.
Give me the potion.

Celia
My lady, much better to
Be brave.

Julia
I'm burning up inside.
What is this potion?

Celia
It's what
Aurelio recommended.

Julia
He must
Have been confused. This is poison.
Celia, help me!

Celia
What is it? I don't
Know what to do.

Julia
I can't breathe. I feel
So weak.

Celia
My lady!

Julia
I feel as if
I'm dying.

Celia

It's all my fault. I wish
I'd never brought the potion!

Julia

You should
Have brought it sooner . . . Find Roselo . . .
Tell him!

Celia

What?

Julia

Tell him I'm his
And his alone. I die for him
So that I cannot belong to someone else.
And tell him not to forget me . . .

Celia

My lady, I need to get you to your room.

Julia

Is this how love must end? At least   100
Roselo is alive. That comforts me.
My father has to know I am
Roselo's wife!

Celia

Madam, be quiet!

Julia

I want the world to know. I shan't be quiet!

Exit **Julia** *and* **Celia**. *Enter* **Fernando**, **Rutilio**, *and
musicians.*

Fernando

This is where you serenade her.

Rutilio

Her beauty is as dazzling as
The sun.

Musician
              A stranger courts her.
He seems to be in favour with
The family. His letters say that he
Adores her.

Fernando
              He's from Verona, is he not?

Musician
    He is.

Fernando
    His name?

Rutilio
              Roselo.

Fernando
                        It sounds
As if heaven favours him.

Rutilio
                    In some
Ways, yes, but on the other hand
No need to envy him. The Capulets
Are on his trail and bent on killing him.
You see, he killed Ottavio. So if
The truth be told, you've got no opposition.

Fernando
In that case, let them sing.

Rutilio
                        No, wait. Someone's
Coming.

Fernando
              They look like strangers.

Enter **Roselo** *and* **Marín**. *They do not see the others.*

Marín
So any success so far?

Roselo

It's early days,   120
Marín. Besides, I'm not so hard
I can forget the other business.

Marín
You mean her getting married!

Roselo

If there
Is any justice in the world, I hope
She pays for it.

Marín

I'm sure she will, sir.

Rutilio (*aside to* **Fernando**)
It's Roselo.

Fernando

Oh, really? Then if
I were a Capulet, I'd seize
This opportunity to take
Revenge.

Rutilio

Come on! Let's ask him what
He's doing here.

Marín (*aside* **to Roselo**)

These people, sir,
Are watching us.

Roselo

Ah, gentlemen!
We've lost our way. We need to find
The main square.

Marín (*aside*)

Well done, sir!

Fernando
You've just walked past it. Down that street!

Roselo
That's very kind of you. Most helpful.

Fernando
Oh, not at all. Let's hope you don't
Get lost again!

Exit **Roselo** *and* **Marín**.

Rutilio
                    Is this supposed
To be the brave Roselo? If so,
His reputation is a joke.

Fernando
He's probably scared because he knows   140
His life's in danger.

Musician
                    So shall we sing
Our song?

Rutilio
          No, wait! Listen!

Fernando
                        The sound
Of swords echoing through the streets.

Rutilio
Let's go and see!

Musician
                Guitars are not
Cut out for this.

Rutilio
              No, true enough.
They'd never make a decent shield.

Musician
I'd rather be at home and put my feet up.

Exit all. Enter **Roselo** *and* **Marín**, *swords drawn*.

Roselo
We made that sound convincing enough.

Marín
They've gone to see what's happening.

Silvia *appears at her window.*

Silvia
You there!

Roselo (*to* **Marín**)
                    I'll tell you later who
They are.

Silvia
                    You there. Can you hear me?

Marín
There's someone at the window, wants
To speak to you.

Roselo
                    My lady, what is it?

Silvia
Who were those people?

Roselo
                              Six good-for-nothings
Beneath the window. We staged a fight
To make them leave, so we could talk
To you.

Silvia
              So who are you?

Roselo
                              Roselo Montague.

Silvia
Then you are welcome. But this is far
Too risky.

Roselo

Madam, the risk is worth it.

Silvia

Tell me the latest gossip.

Roselo

Not gossip, I'm   160
Afraid. It's true. Julia's just got married.

Silvia

Was it arranged?

Roselo

My faith in her
Was quite misplaced. I should have known.
She is, after all, a Capulet.

Silvia

You have my sympathy.

Roselo

Believe
Me, madam, your beauty banishes
My sorrow.

Enter **Anselmo**, *concealed from the others.*

Anselmo

They said I'd find him here.

Marín

Those people. They are coming back.

Roselo

Silvia, don't speak to them.

Silvia

I'll close
The window.

She closes the window and disappears.

Marín

What did you say to her?

Roselo

Oh, this and that! My mood is such,
My life seems at an end.

Marín

Let's go!
There's not much point in staying.

Roselo

No, not when everything displeases me.
Oh, what has Julia done? I love
Her still in spite of her betrayal.

Marín

Look, someone's coming.

Roselo

Let him come
And put an end to all my suffering!

Marín

Who's there?

Anselmo

Who wants to know?

Marín

If you've
No business here, be on your way.   180

Anselmo

Please rest assured. I shan't cause any trouble.
I'm looking for a certain person.

Roselo

I know that voice. Where are you from,
My friend?

Anselmo

Verona. I need to find
A certain gentleman.

Roselo

I think

You've found him, good Anselmo!

Anselmo
Roselo! This is a piece of luck!

Roselo
Indeed it is! What news of Verona?

Anselmo
The most amazing thing you've ever heard.

Roselo
What? Julia's married!

Anselmo
                    No, she isn't.

Roselo
What else can possibly be amazing?

Anselmo
You'll soon find out.

Roselo
                    Then tell me!
Don't keep me in suspense!

Anselmo
                         All right.
Antonio Capulet did all
He could to marry Julia to
The Count of Paris. But neither his
Authority, her uncle's pleas,
Nor all her relatives' persuasion
Could force her to agree to it.
Because of that, her father finally   200
Laid down the law, and so it was
Arranged the wedding would take place
The following day. Imagine, all
The guests were getting dressed; everyone
Was waiting eagerly to see
The Count arrive, when Julia suddenly
Collapsed.

Roselo

      What do you mean?

Anselmo

                  Roselo, please!

Don't interrupt!

Roselo

             Don't interrupt

When Julia's dead?

Anselmo

            She isn't dead!

Be patient!

Roselo

        If she's alive, then I

Live too!

Anselmo

        They grieved for her throughout

The night: her parents, family,

The entire city.

Roselo

          Anselmo, get

To the following day before I die.

Anselmo

At last the next day dawned, but Julia was

As cold as ice and could not speak.

Roselo

Anselmo, your night was tedious but

Your day is even worse. If Julia has

No life, it cannot be day. She *is*

The day.

Anselmo

        And so the day went by,   220

And they, believing she was dead . . .

Roselo
As I am too!

Anselmo
                Arranged the burial
For five o'clock.

Roselo
                When all my hopes
Shall be buried too.

Anselmo
                The funeral was
Magnificent. Small children, boys,
Old men all weeping behind the coffin.

Roselo
So why am I still here when all
I want is death?

Anselmo
                Be patient! Wait!

Roselo
What use is patience? If Julia's in
Her grave, why must I wait?

Anselmo
                                Because
The story is unique.

Roselo
                As is my sorrow!
The fact she didn't marry is
No comfort if she's dead.

Anselmo
                        You have
To hear me out.

Roselo
                What more is there
To listen to?

Anselmo
>   Oh, quite a bit.

Roselo
> Anselmo, you remind me of
> A doctor. Instead of killing me
> With one large dose of medicine,
> You eke it out in smaller measures.

Anselmo
> Stop interrupting. I haven't finished.   240

Roselo
> Go on! I'm listening.

Anselmo
>   Well, then
> Aurelio summoned me and said
> That Julia wrote to him, informing him
> That by the time he'd read the note,
> She would be dead. He acted quickly, made
> A special potion which he gave
> To Celia, and which, when swallowed, has
> The power to induce a two-day sleep
> In which the individual appears to be dead.
> So Julia, thinking that the potion was
> A poison, swallowed it. Aurelio then
> Instructed me to travel here and bring
> You news of this. At present Julia lies
> Inside the family tomb. Aurelio says
> That you should come and rescue her
> And make your way to France or Spain.

Roselo
> Anselmo, this is unbelievable!
> It frightens me. What if she wakes
> And finds herself not only in the dark
> But in the midst of rotting corpses?   260
> She will go mad!

Anselmo
>Aurelio will take care

Of her. Let's go!

Roselo
>I think I was intended as

A model for unhappy lovers.

Marín

Anselmo, wait!

Anselmo
>What is it?

Marín
>Are

There many corpses in the tomb?

Anselmo

Of course. It's full of them.

Marín
>I think,

In that case, I shall wait outside.

Exit **Anselmo**, **Roselo**, *and* **Marín**. *Enter the* **Count of Paris**, *in mourning, and the* **Duke of Verona**.

Paris

I doubt true happiness shall ever come
My way.

Verona
>My dear Count, the wise

Man knows how fickle fortune is.
Just as the tides both ebb and flow,
So are we all exposed to changing fortune,
Our joys and miseries combined.

Paris

If I possessed the greatest treasures in
The world and lost them all, I promise you
I'd laugh at it. But seeing her die,

This girl who would have brought me happiness
Beyond compare, is far too much
For any man. If it had been
A year, a month, a week from now,   280
I would have had some happiness.
But dying as she was about
To take her marriage vows, that is
The worst of all misfortunes, far
Too cruel.

Verona

        But better than a year,
A month, or even a week from now.
By then you would have loved her more,
And so your grief would be much greater.

Paris

As would my joy have been. I know
You want to comfort me, but there
Is nothing you can do to ease my pain.

Enter a servant.

Servant

My lord, Antonio Capulet to see you.

Verona

See how he bears his sorrow. Learn from him.

Enter **Antonio**.

Antonio

I'm not here to complain about
What's happened, nor to win your sympathy.
It's often said that love and death
Were fellow travellers once upon
A time, shared lodgings at an inn,
And then confused their arrows. That's why,
Of course, young men so often die   300
Of love, while it invigorates the old.
It's what has happened to me now.
Ottavio's death means that my brother's house

Has no male heir, and Julia's that
My own will not produce a son.
Because of that my brother has agreed
That I should marry Dorotea,
Despite the difference in our age.
My niece, we are convinced, provides
The only hope of solving our situation.

Paris (*aside*)
It's true there's no fool like an old fool!

Antonio
I'd hoped, of course, that Julia's marriage to
The Count would give me peace of mind
In that respect. But such is life.
We cannot know what lies ahead
Of us. And as for Dorotea, she
Accepts her father's proposition.
As soon as Rome agrees to it,
Our marriage will take place.

Verona
               If this
Is, as you say, the only way   320
To solve the problem of succession, so be it!
Your niece will have in you a husband and
A father. And she will compensate
To some degree at least both Julia's and
Ottavio's deaths.

Paris
            I share those sentiments,
My friend. You are much better equipped
Than I to guarantee succession.

Antonio
I doubt it, my lord. But even so
I felt it only right that you should be
Informed of these developments.

Verona

Which proves you are a man of honour and
Maturity. But where is your wife?
Perhaps you think it safer to keep
Her hidden away.

Antonio

That would be true
Of dubious women. Dorotea is
Most virtuous.

Verona

Nevertheless, it's also true
That age goes hand in hand with fear
Of being cuckolded.

Paris

Undoubtedly.

Antonio

Then you shall see my Dorotea for
Yourselves.

Paris

Indeed we shall. Let's hope   340
That things don't go too badly for you!

Exit **Antonio**, *the* **Count of Paris**, *and the* **Duke of
Verona**. *Enter* **Julia**.

Julia

I can't think where I am! And if
I'm dead, how is it I can speak
And feel? What is this place? Why aren't
There any doors or windows? Why
No light? I think I must be dead.
But if I am, how is it that I speak?
How is it that my flesh still covers me?
What room is this, so silent and
So dark? Of course, it all makes sense.
This is a tomb. And now I feel
These bodies all around me, to right

And left. So if I'm still alive,
Why do I find myself among
The dead? And if, as I recall,
Aurelio's potion ended my life,
How is it that this body's still
Intact and trembles when I mention death?
I see a light. Perhaps I am
In hell, a punishment for love.   360
The light comes nearer. If I'm not dead,
I soon shall die of fright.

Enter **Roselo** *with a lantern, and* **Marín**.

Marín
Master, I'll guard the door. It's much
More sensible.

Roselo
                    No, come with me.
Anselmo stays outside. No need
To be so scared.

Marín
                    Oh, no? You ought
To send a priest in first, with hyssop and
Some holy water.

Roselo
                    Mind the step!

Marín
You mean I'm going in?

Roselo
                              Who pays
Your wages?

Marín
                    Oh, God! Someone's pushed
Me in the back!

Marín *grabs hold of* **Roselo**. *They fall, putting out the light.*

Roselo

              Damn it, Marín!
It's black as pitch!

Julia (*aside*)

              Oh, blessed Virgin, help me!
This seems to be the family tomb.

Roselo

What's that?

Marín

            A voice!

Julia

                The potion must have been
A sleeping-draught. They thought me dead
And so they buried me.

Roselo

                It spoke
Again!

Marín

        Please God, deliver us
From evil!

Roselo

            Here, take this candle to
The second chapel.

Marín

               Why me?

Roselo

                  Go on!

Marín

I can't. I'm rooted to the spot.   380

Roselo

Don't argue! Do it!

Marín

                            Someone's pushed me in
The back again.

Roselo

                  All right, stay here!

Marín

Master, don't leave me on my own!

Roselo

Oh, don't be such a coward!

Julia (*aside*)

The light's gone out, but still I hear
A voice . . . no, voices! Do people speak
When they are dead?

Roselo

                      There it is again!

Marín

If blood seeks out the heart, mine's in
My boots!

Roselo

           It comes from over there.

Marín

A collection of corpses gossiping.

Roselo

What shall we do?

Marín

                Get out of here!

Roselo

Have you found the wall?

Marín

                      No, just the neck
Of a stinking corpse!

Roselo

What else?

Marín

His great
Fat belly and his skull. More like
A donkey's. Oh, God!

Roselo

What is it now?

Marín

I put my finger between two planks . . .

Roselo

And?

Marín

Someone bit it! I'm sure they did.

Roselo

Do you know where Ottavio's buried?

Marín

No, don't remind me! Help me someone!

Roselo

What's wrong?

Marín

I want to confess! I need   400
Forgiveness!

Roselo

What for?

Marín

The fish that went missing
The other day. I ate it all.
And the pears in syrup too.

Roselo

Stop prattling on!

Julia (*aside*)

They're coming nearer. There's nowhere to hide.
You there! Are you dead or alive?

Both men fall.

Marín

Oh, I'm dead!

Roselo

            And I soon shall be!
Did someone hit you?

Marín

                They did. If I
Get out of this, there's no more tombs
For me, nor more tom-foolery!
This corpse is like a buzzing bee,
You think he's coming from the right,
And then he stings you from the left.

Roselo

                        I'll call
Her name. Julia! Julia!

Marín

                Let's hope
It doesn't bring Ottavio to life.
With thirty of his friends!

Roselo

              Julia!
My love!

Julia (*aside*)

           That voice! Is it Ottavio?
I can't be sure. Ottavio!

Marín

              It said
'Ottavio'. They're ganging up on us!

Roselo
I'm not Ottavio.

Julia
                    Who are you?

Roselo
Roselo.

Julia
            Roselo!

Roselo
                    Why do you doubt it?   420

Julia
I need more proof.

Roselo
                    Anselmo told
Me that you took a sleeping-draught
Which made you appear dead. Since everyone's
Convinced it's true, I'm here to take
You from this tomb.

Julia
                    Then tell me what
I gave you the night we met.

Roselo
                        A ring.

Julia
And what did you give me?

Roselo
                        Two jewels set
In gold.

Julia
            And later?

Roselo
                    A pen inlaid

With diamonds.

Julia

How did the note
I wrote you first begin?

Roselo

'My dearest husband'.

Marín

What kind of woman's this? You need
To know if she's alive or dead!
Believe me, master, the strangest creatures live
Among the dead.

Roselo

Leave me, Marín!

Marín

Why? What's the hurry?

Julia

Come to me,
My dearest husband!

Marín

Oh, here we go again!

Roselo

To say I'm not going mad would be
Itself pure madness.

Marín

Best get a move on,
Before it's light!

Roselo

Where can we go?

Julia

My father's estate. We can disguise
Ourselves as peasants. Perhaps in time   440
The need for vengeance will grow less.

Roselo
Your beauty will be recognised.

Julia
Not if they think I'm dead.

Roselo
                    That's true.
Let's go this way.

Marín
          No, wait!

Roselo
              What now?

Marín
I have to be in front. I hate the rear!

Roselo
Let fortune favour us!

Exit **Roselo,** **Julia,** *and* **Marín**. *Enter* **Belardo** *and* **Loreto**.

Loreto
I tell you they are coming here.
I saw them leave.

Belardo
              Gentlefolk here?
The countryside's become the court.

Loreto
The thing is you are so wrapped up
In country matters, harvesting
And pruning and the like, you've not
The slightest interest in a wedding.

Belardo
My boy, I've far too much to do
To be concerned with that. But still,
Whose wedding is it? Why, yesterday,
The only thing I saw was funerals.

Loreto
Ah, well, the wedding has to do
With that.

Belardo
            How come, if everyone's
Still grieving?

Loreto
                  Well, as you know, Antonio's lost   460
His daughter, his brother's lost his son.
That means there's no male heir to carry on
The family line, and so, to try
To make that possible, Antonio's marrying
His brother's daughter, Dorotea.
In other words, the funerals have
Produced a wedding.

Belardo
                  I see. Well, that
Makes sense. As long as afterwards
The girl don't take a shine to some
Good-looking lad, and all their property
Don't vanish in some awful flood
Or storm.

Loreto
            That's true enough, but still,
I can't help thinking she'd be better off
With me.

Belardo
            With you?

Loreto
                  Who else?

Belardo
            I expect you think you'd be well suited.

Loreto
You think she's suited to a bloke

Of sixty-nine she can't get rid of?

Belardo
Call Tamar!

Loreto
   Tamar!

Enter **Tamar**.

Tamar
    You think I'm deaf?

Loreto
He told me to call you.

Tamar
      He didn't tell
You to split my ear-drums!

Loreto
      Oh, don't   480
Get so worked up! One day I want
To see you married.

Tamar
    Me married?

Loreto
You're a woman now. You don't want me
Looking after you.

Tamar (*to* **Belardo**)
     So did you want me, father?

Belardo
The house needs cleaning. Top to bottom.
We're expecting lots of people.

Tamar
But who, if everyone's in mourning?

Belardo
A wedding, Tamar. Julia's father.
He's marrying his brother's daughter.

Tamar

Why here?

Belardo

Until they get the Pope's blessing,
They'd rather it wasn't in Verona.

Tamar

Nobility can do as it sees fit.
As for the work, it's obvious I
Can't do it on my own.

Belardo

I'll get
Two girls to help you out. Loreto,
We'll go and find them. And not a word!

Loreto

Of course not, father. I'm like you –
Discreet.

Belardo

You are, you are. I'm glad
I've brought you up so properly.

Exit **Belardo** *and* **Loreto**.

Tamar

Why, everyone's getting spliced, but everything's   500
The opposite of what it should be.
Young men spend all their time at work
Instead of chasing girls, and old men take
Young girls to bed. But I can't say
I envy Dorotea. I'd rather live
In hope than have a corpse come down on me!

Enter **Roselo**, **Anselmo**, **Julia**, *and* **Marín**, *dressed as peasants and carrying sickles.*

Anselmo

May God protect this house!

Roselo
                      And those
Who live in it! God bless you, lady!

Marín
And bless the bread and wine as well,
Amen.

Julia
           And offer you a man – if you
Have any thoughts of marrying –
Who'll be the envy of all those
Who've tied the knot, and cause all single girls
To weep.

Tamar
           God bless you all! Where are
You from?

Roselo
        Ferrara, lady.

Tamar (*to* **Julia**)
                My dear, why not
Remove your veil?

Julia
          I'd rather not.
We've travelled through the night. My hair's
A mess.

Tamar
        So which of these three men
Is your husband?

Marín
            That's me, of course.

Tamar
I see. (*To* **Julia**.) If that's the case, your taste   520
In men falls short of your looks.
I can't believe that you chose him
Instead of these two!

Julia
                    So which would you
    Have chosen?

Tamar
                    Why, him, undoubtedly.
    He has good looks and, I imagine, lots
    Of spirit.

Roselo
                    Oh, please! My friend has even more
    Of it.

Julia (*aside*)
        This may be just a game,
    But, even so, I feel so jealous.

Tamar
    I have to say, my dear, you do
    Look like my mistress, Julia Capulet.
    But what is it that brings you here?

Anselmo
    We thought you might have work for us.

Tamar
    You'll have to ask my father. He's gone
    To find some girls to help me out.
    We have to get things ready for
    Our master's visit.

Julia
                    You mean he's coming here?

Tamar
    Oh, yes. His daughter's dead and so
    There'll be no heir to the estate. That's why
    He's marrying his niece – to have
    A child by her. And since the Pope   540
    Has still to give permission for
    The marriage, he much prefers it here
    To being in Verona.

Roselo (*aside to* **Julia**)
> What can we do?

Julia (*aside to* **Roselo**)
I've no idea.

Anselmo (*aside to* **Julia**)
> If he gets married, you
Will not inherit and I'll lose Dorotea.
She is my life!

Julia
> God help us all! (*To* **Tamar**.) It seems
We've come in time. I'll help you with
Your work and these two men can help
The others in the fields.

Tamar
> Let's make
A start. You come with me and you
Two leave us.

Julia
> I'll see you later, then.

Roselo (*to* **Julia**)
Goodbye, Marcela.

Anselmo
> Goodbye!

Marín
> This is
Most strange! I wonder where these love
Affairs are taking us?

Exit **Julia**, **Roselo**, **Anselmo**, *and* **Marín**. *Enter* **Antonio**
and **Lucio**.

Antonio
I doubt that they are ready to
Receive us.

Lucio

                Perhaps they weren't expecting us,
My lord.

Antonio

        Tamar!

Tamar

             My lord Antonio!

Antonio

        So is your father expecting me?

Tamar

        He knows that you are getting married.
        Our only worry is it's come   560
        So soon. We aren't prepared.

Antonio

                     This has
To be, Tamar. Dorotea's young
But I am getting old. If I
Delay the wedding for another year,
I might be dead and there would be
No child. The marriage must be now.

Tamar

        Of course. I understand. There can't
        Be courtly etiquette and niceties
        At times like these.

Antonio

               Do I seem very old
To you, Tamar?

Tamar

             Not very old,
My lord. Does not your mirror tell
You what you look like?

Antonio

                 It does, it does.
So get the rooms prepared as soon

As possible.

Tamar (*aside*)
                When old men think
Of age, they are impossible!

Exit **Tamar**.

Antonio
                                Lucio, see
If they've arrived.

Lucio
                        At once, my lord.

Exit **Lucio**.

Antonio
I know that I am being rash,
But all I wish to do is solve
The matter of succession, as other men
Have done. And this before it is   580
Too late and night obliterates
This life of mine.

A noise high up.

                        My God! The heavens
Are crashing down on us! May God
Protect me!

Julia, *unseen, above.*

Julia
            Father!

Antonio
                        I know that voice!

Julia
    Father!

Antonio
            Julia! Perhaps I imagine it!

Julia
Listen to what I have to say, even if
I'm from beyond the grave.

Antonio
                              Julia!
Is that you?

Julia
              You ought to know my voice.
Have you forgotten me?

Antonio
                              Where are
You? What do you want?

Julia
                              I come
To speak to you, from far away,
The other world.

Antonio
                  It saddens me
I cannot see you.

Julia
                  You wouldn't want
To see me as I am, cut down
By death.

Antonio
              No, daughter. I couldn't bear
It. Tell me what you've come to say!

Julia
I killed myself because of you!

Antonio
I don't know what you mean.

Julia
                              You tried
To force me into marriage.

Antonio

I meant
It for the best.

Julia

I didn't love   600
The Count, deserving as he was.
And more than that, I was already married.

Antonio

I'm not to blame for you not telling me.
If you had only said: 'Father,
I've married against your wishes,
I couldn't help myself,' I would
Have understood. A girl as sensible
And virtuous as you would never make
A foolish choice.

Julia

I would have told
You, had it been another man.
Aurelio married us, two months ago.

Antonio

And no one knew the truth?

Julia

It was
Too dangerous. And then, because
You wanted to arrange my marriage to
The Count, I killed myself. What else
Was I to do? But now I understand
That you are getting married too,
And so I wish you both a happy life.
As for myself, I have but one request,
Which is that you respect and do   620
Not harm my husband who still lives.
For if you do, I promise you your days
And nights will be a living hell.

Antonio
Then tell me who this husband is.

Julia
The man who killed Ottavio, the son
Of your mortal enemy. In short,
Roselo.

Antonio
                    Daughter, wait! Who would
Have thought? Roselo! The mere mention of
His name offends me. But now she has
My word that I'll respect him, and treat
Him as my son as long as I shall live!

Enter **Teobaldo**, **Dorotea**, *the* **Count of Paris**, **Belardo**,
soldiers. **Anselmo**, **Roselo**, *and* **Marín** *are prisoners.*

Teobaldo
Keep moving, all of you!

Antonio
                              What's going on?

Teobaldo
The heavens have smiled on us.

Antonio
                                        Who are
These people?

Teobaldo
                    Can't you see? This one's
Roselo.

Antonio
        I don't believe it!

Teobaldo
                              Oh, yes!
Roselo Montague in peasant dress.
My people spotted him. I could
Have had him killed but thought it best

To hand him over, together with
His two companions. Belardo here   640
Can be excused for keeping them on
The estate. He'd no idea who he was.

Belardo
Believe me, if I'd known, you'd have
No need to kill him now.

Teobaldo
                                        So how
Shall it be done? What if we tie
Him to a tree and fill the wretch
With arrows or with shot? Just tell
Me which. Why hesitate?

Antonio
                              There's something you
Should know.

Teobaldo
                    Speak up! How shall he die?

Antonio
He cannot die. He has to live.
A little while ago, my daughter's ghost
Appeared. She said Roselo is her husband.

Teobaldo
I don't believe it!

Antonio
                          And to avoid
Her marriage to the Count, she killed
Herself with poison. She also said
That if I persecute Roselo, I
Shall suffer as she does now.

Teobaldo
                                    But you're
Imagining these things. You feel
Responsible for Julia's death.

Antonio

Brother, if you ignore her words,   660
You'll suffer too. Who knows what punishments
She has in mind?

Teobaldo

Stuff and nonsense!

Antonio

Listen! I have a plan. Roselo was
My son-in-law, but now he can
Be yours, by marriage to Dorotea.
I'll stand aside. It's much more satisfactory.

Teobaldo

My daughter marry him? You must
Be mad!

Antonio

It will bring peace to both
The warring families.

Paris

I do believe
This is heaven's will. It cannot be
Denied, Teobaldo. Your daughter has
To marry Roselo.

Teobaldo

Then I have no
Alternative. She shall be his.

Enter **Julia**.

Julia

I think not! He cannot have two wives!

Dorotea

Julia!

Teobaldo

What is all this?

Julia
                            No, stay!
Don't turn away from me! I'm not
A ghost! Father, look at me!

Teobaldo
                            Just tell
Us what you want.

Julia
                    Believe me! I'm not dead!

Antonio
A living soul, no more. And come
To haunt us!

Julia
                    I didn't die. The poison was   680
A sleeping-draught. Roselo brought
Me here. He's with me now. Tell them, Roselo.

Roselo
It's true. I took her from the tomb,
And so she is my wife a second time.

Paris
And justly so. They are well suited to
Each other.

Antonio
                Julia, you have my blessing.
You too, Roselo.

Julia
                Father, Dorotea has
To marry whom she pleases.

Teobaldo
                            So who
Is that?

Julia
        Anselmo.

Anselmo

                  I need to tell
You why I merit her.

Antonio

                    No time
To waste. She is your wife!

Marín

                      And what
About me? Don't I get some reward
For rescuing the corpse?

Julia

                   Of course
You do! A thousand ducats . . . and Celia too,
For good measure! For as they say,
All's well that ends well.

Cleopatra

Francisco de Rojas Zorrilla

Characters

Cleopatra, *Queen of Alexandria*
Mark Antony, *a Roman general*
Octavian, *a Roman general*
Lepidus, *a Roman general*
Irene, *Octavian's sister*
Lelio, *adviser to Cleopatra*
Alligator, *a Roman soldier*
Libia, *Cleopatra's servant*
Octavius, *a Roman captain*
A Woman
Soldiers

Act One

Enter **Irene** *and* **Lepidus**.

Irene
You are so tiresome, Lepidus.

Lepidus
But you know how much I love you, Irene.

Irene
Even though I make you suffer?

Lepidus
Your coldness inflames my love the more.

Irene
Then what if I say that I despise you?

Lepidus
It does not make me love you less.

Irene
They say that for a fool such coldness has
A certain sweetness. Where there is love,
I understand how such disdain
May seem a gift. But surely not
Where there is only hate. If I
Despise and hate you, then, you must
Admit that what till now inflamed
Your love must cool it.

Lepidus
                    Am I to think
You do not love me?

Irene
                   Oh, no, sweet Lepidus, I
Despise you.

Lepidus
              Is not to love the same
As to despise?

Irene

> There *is* a difference. Not
To love is one thing. To love so harshly quite
Another.

Lepidus

> You do not love me, then?

Irene

Quite true!

Lepidus

> You hate me!

Irene

> Truer still!   20

Lepidus

I can't believe the words of love
That came from those sweet lips were not
Dictated by your heart. Why don't
You love me?

Irene

> I cannot love a man
Who has surrendered to another woman.

Lepidus

The fate of any man owes less
To bravery than fickle fortune.
Cleopatra overwhelmed me. In any case,
I do believe that, were I not
The victim of her sword, I would
Have fallen to her dazzling beauty.

Irene

Enough! A man may take revenge
As a lover, but not by vulgarly praising another.
When I told you I despised you, did
I say that I loved someone else?
I know your game. You think this praise
Of someone else will melt my coldness.

I promise you that it will not.
It will not do to answer my disdain
With mere coarseness.

Lepidus

My praise   40
Of her, considered well, is but
My way of saying how much lovelier
You are, which makes me love you all
The more. How can I then offend
You if my praise of her, devoid
Of any love, is but designed
To tell you that in every way
You are superior?

Irene

I hate Cleopatra.
I will not have you pay
Her compliments.

Lepidus

But you despise me.

Irene

As you offend me.

Lepidus

How can I when
Your thoughts are with Mark Antony?

Irene

Poor Lepidus! I do believe
That you are jealous.

Lepidus

And I believe
That you're in love with him.

Irene

Have I
Said anything to that effect?

Lepidus
Deny that you prefer him.

Irene
He is
Extremely handsome, bold and clever . . .

Lepidus
And I have been acclaimed three times
By Rome for deeds much bolder still.   60

Irene
In spite of which Cleopatra bends
You to her fickle will.

Lepidus
She is
So beautiful. No man can resist her.

Irene
You are becoming coarse again.

Lepidus
And so are you when you persist
In praising Antony.

Irene
I must
Admit, my words are somewhat careless,
Obedient to desire.

Lepidus
Then you
Should not be angry if my eyes
Were dazzled by the lovely Cleopatra.

Irene
How dare you! I shall hear no more!

Lepidus
How very difficult women are!

Sound of trumpets, answered by trumpets with mutes.

Irene

What trumpets pierce the air with these
Bright sounds?

Lepidus

What dull and muted sounds
Are these that answer them?

Irene

An army there
Returns in triumph.

Lepidus

Another there,
But in defeat.

Irene (*aside*)

I pray the one
Victorious is Mark Antony!
Octavian is my brother, true, but in
My heart my lover means much more to me.   80

Lepidus (*aside*)

Heaven grant Mark Antony's the one
Defeated! Although he is my friend,
No friend means more than my sweet lady.

Irene (*aside*)

I'll let discretion rule my feelings.
Let's go and welcome them.

Lepidus

I shall
Be first in paying homage to these two
Great men, these worthy sons of Rome.

Irene

And I, though unaccustomed to
The sounds of war, shall be your rival.

Enter **Mark Antony** *and* **Octavian**.

Octavian
Lepidus! How good to see you!

Lepidus
Welcome, Octavian!

Antony
                        Irene, more beautiful
Than ever!

Irene
            My lord, Mark Antony!
What news of the campaign?

Antony
                              A quite
Resounding victory.

Lepidus
                  What news,
Octavian? Why so silent?

Octavian
                        What can
I say? A bitter defeat.

Irene
                  Great Mars
Has favoured you, my lord.

Antony
                        I need
To speak to Octavian.

Octavian
                        I wish to greet
Mark Antony.

Antony
            Lepidus, my dear friend!

Irene
My dear brother, welcome home!   100

Octavian
Antony, why so downhearted?

Antony
                              I
Am saddened by your fate, yet you
Seem cheerful.

Octavian
                    Happy for you, my friend,
Rejoicing in your triumph.

Antony
                              Which is
As nothing in the light of your defeat.
It makes me sad.

Octavian
                    As I am glad
For your victory.

Antony
                    You are
The truest friend, Octavian.

Octavian
                         Describe
What happened.

Antony
                    When you have told me
Of your exploits.

Octavian
                    You will recall
The day when, fired by ambition, we all
Set out, intent on conquering
The world.

Antony
                I set my sights on Asia.

Octavian

I

Europe.

Lepidus

I Africa.

Octavian

All three of us, loyal and
Devoted friends, forming the great
Triumvirate of Rome.

Lepidus

You know
How I, by some malevolent fate,
Was defeated at sea by Cleopatra.

Antony

How I, receiving news of that defeat,   120
Abandoned Asia in the hope
Of helping you.

Octavian

And I Europe.
I was the first to arrive,
My plan to capture Alexandria,
And Cleopatra with it.

Antony

On which
Account I made for Asia once
Again.

Lepidus

And I had, by that time, returned
To Rome, ashamed of my defeat.

Octavian

This is what happened. We sailed as dawn
Began to break, the morning star
Greeting the sun as it awakened from
Its sleep. Three hundred ships pierced

The sea-green mist of morning, each
A centaur upon the waves, in flight
Half-bird, in skimming the foam half-fish.

Antony
Our journey commenced as night began
To fall, and as the silver moon appeared in
The heavens, putting the sun to flight.
Three thousand men in all, each trained   140
And hardened in the art of war.

Octavian
We headed west when suddenly
A mist began to form, as though
Great clouds were coming from the sea
Itself. The sky grew dark, the wind
Blew fiercely, the sun was hidden by
The clouds, the waves whipped up as if
The elements themselves were now at war.
On board our ships we could
Not see, such was the darkness which
Enveloped us. For some it was
A blessing, obscuring the danger all
Around, while others welcomed it
As proof of their greater courage.
And some, their minds abandoned to
Their fears, and thinking that the masts
They saw were trees, jumped into the sea,
Believing it was land.

Antony
I do believe that fortune favoured us.
Our thirst was quenched by silver streams.   160
The trees provided fruit and, when
The summer's day grew hot, most welcome shade.
The birds, when we were tired, soothed
Our ears with pleasing harmony,
The green and pleasant land our eyes.
In short, it was as if we had
Been truly blessed by destiny.

Octavian
    At last the fierce storm subsided.
We journeyed on and finally
Reached Alexandria, a town where even
The sun is dazzled by
The lovely eyes of Cleopatra.
We disembarked, but hardly had
We reached the shore, than she
Attacked us, as if to prove the point
That beauty cannot be divorced
From cunning. My men attempted to
Withdraw, but she, on seeing this,
Attacked again, and water which
Was crystal-clear was soon bright red   180
With blood. The spectacle was one
Of total carnage. A soldier there
Bore on his back the body of
Another. A second, bleeding from
His wounds, attempted to revive
Himself, drinking the blood of one
Who was already dead. A third in flight
Encountered death, a just reward
For cowardice, but he who stood
His ground to prove his bravery
Died just the same, the coward's and
The hero's fate as one, all equal in
The eyes of death.

Antony
                My own campaign was with
The king of Persia. The king himself
Was fiercely arrayed in skins, his troops
Preceded by majestic elephants,
Which in their bulk were moving castles topped
By bright red flags.
My men advanced, inspired by
The wish to overcome such odds.   200
Our first attacks were unsuccessful,
Our soldiers brutally forced back,

Our battle-lines divided by
The onslaught of those mighty beasts,
Which on their backs bore soldiers by
The dozen. The elephants advanced
Implacably, but I knew well
That if they were to trip and fall,
Such is their weight they would not rise
Again. And so we dug a ditch,
Filled to the brim with sand, and they,
Arriving there, were trapped in it,
Both beast and man quite powerless.

Octavian
A horse which seemed more like a bird
Was Cleopatra's mount. It skimmed
The foam and yet, for all its pride,
Obeyed its rider who outshone the dawn
In all its beauty. Her troops, encouraged by
Her valour, drove us back towards
The sea. I sought the safety of   220
Our ships and tried to rescue those
Who, it would seem, preferred to die,
While those who had been rescued thought
That they, in their shame, were better dead.

Antony
The Persian king was overcome,
And I myself acclaimed as king
By all his people.

Octavian
                    And I set sail
For home again, defeated by
The brave and lovely Cleopatra.

Antony
The heavens proclaimed my victory.

Octavian
The ocean my defeat.

Antony

                        In spite
Of which, I, not you, believe myself
The loser.

Octavian

                    And I, rejoicing in your triumph,
Regard myself the victor.

Antony

                            My friend,
The world proclaims your illustrious name.

Octavian

And celebrates your fame and reputation.

Antony

So men in future times may say
We both were true and faithful comrades.

Octavian *and* **Lepidus** *together*

If only we, Mark Antony,
Could equal you in fortune and success.   240

Antony

I promise you, Octavian, my success
Shall soon be yours. You shall once more
Be favoured by the gods, for though my men
Have only just returned from long
Campaigns, I swear revenge on Cleopatra.
This steel, now blunt, shall once again
Be stained with foreign blood. The kingdoms I
Had planned to overcome will be obliged
To wait, while I take vengeance on
A mere woman. Lepidus, if fate
Has been the architect of your defeat,
And you, Octavian, have been less
The victim of your courage than
Your destiny, I promise you
That in your names I seek
This glorious victory. I shall

Not rest till it has been achieved,
Nor shall my men. We shall set sail.
Our speedy ships, like ploughs, shall make
Great furrows in the sea, which we   260
Shall sow with Cleopatra's blood.
I cannot wait to see what mystery
It is that valour cannot overcome.
Let's go.

He makes to depart.

Octavian

      Antony, wait!
There is a promise I must keep.
You will recall we both agreed
That if you now returned
Victorious, my sister Irene would be
Your wife. The victory is yours,
To keep my word the smallest of favours.
Let the marriage take place before you leave.

Lepidus

If I may speak, Octavian, that will delay
The vengeance which we both aspire to.
When Antony is ready to depart
On our behalf, you try to stop him.
Much better to let him go. Since when
Are the demands of war of less
Importance than the sweet delights
Of love?

Antony

      You are both right, my friends.
Lepidus, I take your advice, and thank   280
You, Octavian, for this favour. I accept
Yet do not accept it, which is to say
That you, Irene, shall be my wife.
But for the moment love must wait,
The pleasures of the marriage-bed
Second to the harsh requirements of war.

I shall first defeat this Cleopatra,
But be obliged, while I'm away,
To your love and your friendship.

Lepidus (*aside*)
I scarcely contain my jealousy.

Antony
Lepidus, advise my men that soon
We shall be ready to embark
For Africa.

Lepidus
      It shall be done.
(*Aside.*) And may the gods grant me one favour:
That in what lies ahead Mark Antony
Shall be the loser.

Exit **Lepidus**.

Octavian
Irene, leave us. I have
A private matter to discuss
With Antony.

Irene
      Of course. I only wish
That he who rules my heart were more   300
Inclined to love than war.

Exit **Irene**.

Antony
Well? What can it be, this private matter?

Octavian
It is quite difficult. I find
It quite embarrassing. My words
Stick in my throat.

Antony
      Have courage, Octavian.

Octavian
It is not easy to be bold
When what I have to say is proof
Of cowardice.

Antony
                    I can't think what
You mean. You aren't the kind of man
To run away from danger.

Octavian
                              It's even worse.

Antony
I don't believe it.

Octavian
                    The fact is, when
I first set eyes on Cleopatra . . .

Antony
You were attracted by her beauty!

Octavian
If only that were so! I was
Attracted, as you say, but in
The palette of our feelings attraction is
A common colour which, depending on
The circumstances, may become
More vivid or more pale.

Antony
                        And in your case?

Octavian
More vivid. I am obsessed by her.   320
The colour is ingrained in me.
No painter in the world could hope,
However skilled, to modify
Its tones, not least the darker colours of
Despair and absence. When I first saw her,
My eyes traversed the lovely ocean of

Her hair. I drowned in its sheer beauty,
And asked myself how eyes as clear
And calm as hers could be the cause
Of tempests such as those which rage
Within the hearts of men. I am
The one who, mocking love, am mocked
By it. Not only was I beaten on
The battlefield. She overcame
Me too where love's concerned, my heart
Surrendered to her perfect beauty.
You are my friend, Mark Antony,
My brother too, and now you leave
To conquer Cleopatra. Good fortune smiles
On you, and makes of me an object of   340
Its own inconstancy. You are
Most favoured by the stars, while I
Contend with Venus, Mars and Jupiter,
Such is my own unhappy fate.
I only ask one thing, which will
Restore my fortune and my happiness.
Defeat Cleopatra; overcome
The kingdom of those eyes to whom
Cupid himself, though blind, pays tribute.
When this has been achieved,
Her territory can be yours,
Her beauty mine. Since we have always shared
Whatever kingdoms we have won,
We'll do so once again, but you
Shall have her country and her wealth,
And I the woman who means more
To me than any wealth you can
Imagine. Are we agreed?

Antony

I was distressed by your defeat,
But now confess I am the more   360
Distressed to see you overcome
By love. How can the man whose fame
And bravery resound throughout

The world become a prisoner
Of passion's chains? My dear Octavian,
You must control yourself.

Octavian

Irene is already yours.
On that account you can afford to be
So temperate and in control
Of your desires.

Antony

Octavian, love
And valour are extremes, and thus
The source of strong emotions. But in
My view love is the lesser of the two,
The more indulgent, weakening
A man's resolve, while valour is
The greatest virtue. You know the truth of this.

Octavian

I cannot agree.

Antony

Put valour first.

Octavian

I cannot, in spite of everything
You say.

Antony

You think her more important?

Octavian

She is unlike any other woman: 380
A goddess I adore.

Antony

There is,
Then, no escape from her?

Octavian

I fear, none.

Antony

It seems, then, you are deaf to my
Advice and cannot help yourself
Where she's concerned. But I shall not
Go back on what I've said. When I
Have conquered her, you'll have her for
Yourself, this woman who's become
The centre of your universe,
The object of your dreams. Command
My men. We'll soon be setting sail.
I promise you, my friend, that I
Shall not return to Rome until,
In recognition of the man
You are, commander of one half
Of this entire world, I can give
You Cleopatra.

Octavian

My friend for ever!

Antony

We are as brothers.

Octavian

Promise me
You'll keep your word that Cleopatra shall
Be mine.

Antony

Ask and I'll give you the sun   400
Itself.

Octavian

My love is reward for such
True loyalty. May the gods protect you.
Meanwhile, I live in hope.

Antony

And I
Favoured by good fortune. You must
Be patient.

Enter **Irene** *and* **Lepidus** *from opposite sides of the stage.*

Irene
> The trumpets sound. The soldiers now
> Prepare to leave.

Lepidus
> Accompanied by drums, harsh instruments
> Of war.

Antony
> My dear Irene.

Irene
> Let me embrace you. My soul goes with you.

They embrace.

> May the gods allow you to return to me.

Antony
> The gods, I think, shall favour me. Goodbye,
> Lepidus.

Lepidus
> May they guarantee your safe
> Return.

Octavian
> Antony, do not forget
> Your promise.

Antony
> How could I when you always
> Remind me?

Irene
> I don't know why
> I am so afraid.

Antony
> You must not fear.

Irene
> I love you so much.

Antony

If, within a year,
No news has come of my success,
You may conclude my courage has been   420
In vain, that I have been abandoned by
Good fortune. Come then to my
Assistance.

Lepidus

I give you my word.

Octavian

As I do too.

Irene

And I'll accompany both
Of them.

Antony

I agree to that and say
Farewell.

Irene

The gods be with you, Antony.

Lepidus (*aside*)

And may my rival rot in hell!

Exit all. Enter **Alligator**.

Alligator

I'm just a poor Roman, you know.
I came here with Octavian, full
Of confidence I'd show these foreigners
A thing or two. Well, we took them on
All right, but what we didn't know
Is that these Egyptians fight
Like demons. To tell the truth,
My sword felt like a piece of lead,
And so I thought it best to put my faith
In these two feet. In short, I ran
For it! Oh, yes, I know it's not

The thing to do, not for a soldier anyway.
But ever since, just take my word,   440
Everything's gone much better than
I thought it would. Octavian wasn't pleased,
As you can well imagine.
He said to me: 'If you are killed,
The world will celebrate your fame.'
I said to him: 'Fancy that! I'd rather live,
If you don't mind, and have no name
To celebrate!' I mean what fool lays down
His life so those who live can tell
How brave he was? Who cares about
Posterity if what it means
Is you, poor sod, are just past history?
In any case I chose to live.
I saw how bloody things had got
And sought safe refuge in these mountains.
The Romans gone, I stayed behind
In Alexandria, safe enough,
Since no one knows me here, but at
The same time poor. I need a job, then.
Not any job, mind, but something that   460
Befits my station, that can bring
Some money in, and keep me in
The style I am accustomed to.
I've always fancied doctoring.
They have it made, those doctors! Who else
Can bury his mistakes together with
His customers? Not only that!
You must have heard the neighbours say:
'She's been under the doctor the last
Three months.' So, a profession and
Position much to be desired, not
To mention a tonic in itself.
I could be a lawyer, I suppose.
I'd fancy wearing wig and gown,
And being in court and walking up
And down before the judge, trying

To impress the jury. Oh, yes, they make
A pile of money out of that.
Whoever said that crime doesn't pay?
And don't they charge fantastic fees   480
So they can eat from plates of silver,
Concealing their hypocrisy,
While innocent men are left to rot
For years in jail? Still, most of all
I'd love to be an apothecary.
You won't believe the things that they
Get up to, mixing their magic potions.
You know that yellow medicine
You take for coughs? The colour gives
You some idea where it comes from.
I shan't say any more, except
That its ingredients aren't what you
Might call divine – in fact that's a rhyme
For what it comes from.
If I were an apothecary,
I'd make good use of candle-grease.
And put it in my creams and ointments,
Or crush up flies and other such-
Like creatures. Mixed well they'd make
A beautiful concoction, not least   500
To help you ladies there, if you suffer from
A poor complexion. And I, meanwhile,
Would make a fortune, which, after all,
Is my true ambition.

Enter **Libia**.

Libia

                              Let the gods take revenge
On Cleopatra for what she's done.
She's issued this decree,
Which says that no one in her kingdom
Should have sex. Can you believe it?
Forbidding the very thing
That Nature itself would have us do?

Consider all the creatures
On land and sea: they all do what
Comes naturally, so why must we
Be different just because of her?
To tell the truth, since she made love
Illegal, I fancy it more than
I ever did. There's not a man
That I don't find attractive,
No matter what his faults!
This cross-eyed fellow, he was winking   520
At someone else, you see, but since
I thought he was winking at me, I had
Him by mistake. I don't object to bald
Men either. I know some women do,
But I say, if he gives you pleasure,
It isn't his head that really matters.
I even take to ugly ones,
Pretending they look better than
They do. I tell myself a short
Man's tall, a fat one thin. I mean,
You can't have everything you want,
Now can you? So better make the most
Of it, convince yourself that beauty's in
The eye of the beholder. As for
This so-called queen, Cleopatra,
Her orders are that any wife
Caught shagging someone other than
Her husband must be burned alive.
And any girl caught doing it must first
Be put to death, then burned. I ask   540
You, is that really fair? If they've
Already burned us here, how can
They burn us there in hell as well?
It makes you think! Though thinking doesn't damp
My ardour. In fact, my lust is greater than
Before. I say: 'Lust now, pay later!'
The day of reckoning comes soon.
Enough.

Alligator

      This woman's handsome!
I'll try to impress her!

Libia

                This fellow's keen,
I reckon.

Alligator

      Get on with it! What am
I waiting for?

Libia

      I'll speak to him,
Though I may burn for it!

Alligator

                Jupiter
Be praised!

Libia

      For ever and ever, amen!
(*Aside.*) I'd better make the most of this!

Alligator

Pretty lady, would you give a man
Who's shy a chance to speak to you?

Libia

You've got it.

Alligator

      You are most considerate.

Libia

Come closer. Don't be shy!

Alligator

                May the gods
Reward such charity!

Libia

              Take my hand.

She holds out her hand.

Alligator

And Cupid such generosity!   560
It's three months since I've had a bite
To eat. But since you offer me
This morsel, I'll take a mouthful.

Libia

You're welcome.

She embraces him.

Alligator

You are a most obliging mouthful . . . I
Mean soul.

Libia

                And a sinner with it.

Alligator

                                    I don't
Quite follow.

Libia

                It doesn't matter. I fancy you.

Alligator

I can't believe it.

Libia

                The thought of being
Deprived makes me want it all the more.

Alligator

I'll have the greatest respect
For you. I'll be a true and honest lover.

Libia

Let's hope that I don't burn for it.

Alligator

I'll do my best to light your fire.

Libia
> I don't mean that. They've passed a law
> Forbidding sex. The punishment
> Is being burned.

Alligator
> So let's burn now
> As well as afterwards. Are men
> Included in this punishment?

Libia
> No,
> They aren't.

Alligator
> You mean only women?

Libia
> So
> It seems.

Alligator
> That's what I call a dream
> Scenario.

Libia
> You selfish creature! How can   580
> You say you love me if you'd see
> Me burn?

Alligator
> But I don't want to see
> You burn, at least . . .

Libia
> What?

Alligator
> Not till afterwards!

Voices (*off*)
> Make way! Make way!

Alligator
It's Queen Cleopatra. On her way to
The Amphitheatre.

Libia
                    I've decided I
Don't love you.

Alligator
                    And I've decided I
Love you.

Libia
          I don't even know your name.

Alligator
Alligator.

Libia
        What?

Alligator
              Alligator.

Libia
                    Oh, well,
In that case, I'll see you later.

Exit **Libia**. *Enter* **Cleopatra**. **Lelio** *(an old man), soldiers and followers.*

Lelio
Queen of Egypt, brightest sun
Of Alexandria! Who can compare
With your greatness or your beauty?
Who else is there who so combines
Such dazzling looks with so much prudence?
You alone have conquered love, resisting it
Despite that loveliness that makes
All men obliged to pay you homage.
Why, even the eagle that dares fly near the sun
Is blinded by the brightness of   600
Your eyes. The perfect rose . . .

Cleopatra

Enough!
This praise is most excessive. Why
Always praise my beauty? I'd much
Prefer you speak of other things,
Especially my courage and my valour.
Why must you give priority
To qualities which you consider more
Becoming of a woman than a man?
Did I not conquer Lepidus?
Did I not turn the ocean red
With blood and reduce his mighty ships
To mere matchwood? And what of proud
Octavian? Did I not overcome
Him on this very shore, destroy
His fleet and put his men to flight?
I did! And still you praise
My beauty rather than my bravery.
I now await Mark Antony,
This general whose courage is
Acclaimed throughout the world. He too   620
Shall end up on my sword and be
A further proof that, though I am
A woman in appearance, my spirit is
As strong as that of any man.
I shall not listen further
To anyone who praises the beauty of
These eyes. I'd rather tear them out
Than hear such flattery. And if
It's said the sun itself is jealous of
Their light, I'd rather stare at it
And let myself go blind, so that
My eyes would not possess such brightness.
My one regret is to be born
A woman and be obliged to act
As women do. If only I could change
My nature!

Lelio
                    Your majesty, please
    Be seated. The city pays you homage.
    Your subjects celebrate your victories.
    Let your judgements now be ruled more
    By pity than by harshness.   640

Cleopatra
    Provided that the law of chastity
    Has not been broken. What have we here?

She sits.

Lelio
    Two contrary claims, your majesty.
    Two men quite different from each other.
    The first we have arrested. It seems
    He falls in love with any woman he
    Sets eyes on. He asks you punish him.
    The other says you should reward him.
    His claim is that, throughout his life,
    He has not spoken to any woman,
    And thus avoids temptation, obedient to
    Your law of chastity.

Cleopatra
                        We have,
    Then, two extremes: a man who claims
    He loves all women, and one who says
    He's never loved a single one.

Lelio
    Indeed, your majesty. Your judgement is
    Awaited.

Cleopatra
                Then free the one who's been
    Arrested and seize the one who is
    Still free. A man who claims he loves
    All women cannot love at all,   660
    And he who boasts he's never loved

Conceals, I think, a secret love
Which breaks my law of chastity.
He is a hypocrite who must
Be punished; the other is pathetic. Set
Him free.

Lelio

       The next case is a man
Condemned to death for slander.

Cleopatra

                     Whom does
He slander?

Lelio

        Yourself, your majesty.
He says that you are generous
Merely because you want the world
To think you are. He claims as well,
That what to you seems just
Is nothing more than cruelty;
That you are proud, impatient too,
Excessively ambitious, and such
Success as you enjoy is more
To do with luck than valour.

Cleopatra

This man has courage. Does he
Speak well of anyone?

Lelio

           No, he
Does not. He pours abuse on everyone.   680

Cleopatra

Then I commute his sentence, if what
He says of me is also what
He says of others. Release him, but
On one condition. He shall be put
To death if he is ever found
To sing my praises. It will not do

To have a man speak well of me
If he speaks only ill of others.
It smacks of too much flattery.

Alligator

Your majesty, if I may speak.
If you reward the man who thought
You'd punish him, I'll be your servant.
You won't believe how ill I'll speak
Of you. Your name shall be my doormat. Will
You have me?

Cleopatra

What office would you have?

Alligator

I'll be your fool. The office suits me.

Cleopatra

Where are you from?

Alligator

I'm a Roman, madam,
But much prefer to be an Egyptian.

Cleopatra

What brought you to Alexandria?

Alligator

Not what, but who, your majesty.   700
It was Caesar Octavian.

Cleopatra

You were lost
In the battle?

Alligator

Just a little
At first, it's true. But then I found
Myself. I ran away from you and hid.

Cleopatra

How exactly?

Alligator
> To be precise, I used
My feet.

Cleopatra
> You mean you are a coward?

Alligator
Only a little one. But better
A little one than a big one, eh?

Enter a veiled **Woman**.

Lelio
Your majesty, this woman has
Been sentenced to be burned.
She was discovered with a man
And so defies your law. The offence
Is proved.

Cleopatra
> Then why delay? Burn her!

Woman
Your majesty, have mercy on
A poor woman! I love the man,
As he loves me. I gave myself
To him because we shall be married soon.
I have his word. I beg you show
Compassion.

Cleopatra
> You should have waited. Now
It is too late.

Lelio
> If I may speak,   720
Your majesty, the lady is
Of noble birth. This punishment
Will bring disgrace upon her family.
Is there no way you can show
Her pity?

Cleopatra
> The field you see in front
Of you is full of asps. Take two
Of them and let them coil themselves
Around this lustful creature's arms.
Their poison shall prove stronger still
Than that of love, their sweet embrace
More deadly. If she is not to burn,
This is the punishment I choose.
Her blood shall burn more painfully
Than it has ever done on love's
Account.

Woman
> If I must die, I beg
The gods take vengeance on this tyrant queen
And give me justice. May you die too,
The victim of a deadly asp,
And may you too, before you die,
Become infected by love's poison.   740

Cleopatra
> My fate shall not be yours. Your death
Is just. Take her away.

Woman
> I curse you!
Let your end be mine! May you too feel
Love's pain and then condemn yourself to death,
The best example of your punishment.

Exit the **Woman**. *Sound of trumpets.*

Cleopatra
> What are these sounds? Who comes?

Lelio
> See there.
A fleet of ships. I'd say two hundred at
The very least. They seem like gulls
That skim the waves, or fish that pierce

The air. And at their head a ship
Which, more a bird of pine than feathers, turns
The bright blue water into snow-white foam.
Its stern displays red flags that gleam
Like rubies in the sun. Its prow
Adorned with ivory, its oars
With silver, its rudder gold, it rivals
The sun in all its splendour.

All

It gathers in the sails.

Lelio

And puts down anchor. A soldier
Approaches along the sand.

Cleopatra

                        More fool   760
Than soldier! He shall feel my anger!
Let him tell us who he is.

Voices (*off*)

                        All hail,
Mark Antony! All hail!

Cleopatra

                        The name
Strikes fear in my heart, and yet,
One must feel fear to be brave.
I shall conceal my face. I want
This man to be defeated by
My sword, not by my beauty.

She covers her face with a veil. Enter **Mark Antony**.

Antony

Queen Cleopatra, may the heavens protect
You!

Cleopatra

        Please leave us.

Lelio *and* **Alligator** *leave.* **Mark Antony** *and* **Cleopatra**
avoid each other's gaze.

Cleopatra

I beg
You, please be seated.

Antony

They say the world
Acclaims your beauty more than your valour,
Yet that will not avail you now.
I come to take away from you
This kingdom that you rule. Alexandria shall
Be mine as from today and you
My prisoner.

Cleopatra

Who would have thought
The great Mark Antony could say
Such foolish things? Your bravery
No doubt impresses cowards, as does   780
Your clarion call my poor subjects.
But I am not impressed. In fact,
I promise you that I, not you,
Will soon command the whole of Asia.
I recommend you once again
Set sail or you shall be
My prisoner. Have you forgotten how
I conquered Lepidus?

Antony

He blames
The sea, which swallowed eighty of
His ships.

Cleopatra

What does Octavian say?

Antony

That he surrendered only to
The beauty of your eyes.

Cleopatra
                              Which is
Precisely why you shall not see them.
For then, when I have overcome,
You cannot claim my eyes defeated you.

Antony
Were I to see them, I know
I would not yield to their beauty.

Cleopatra
I look away because I know
That you could not resist it.

Antony
                                   I do
The same. For you to look at me
Would fill your heart with fear.   800

Cleopatra
You fear my beauty more than I
Your valour.

Antony
                    Not if you were the sun
Itself in all its splendour!

Cleopatra
                         Then look
At me!

She uncovers her face. They look at each other.

Antony
            Your eyes destroy me!

Cleopatra
                              Turn
Away! I see in you the image of
My death.

Antony
            And I in you the image of

My life.

Cleopatra
> I look at you and yet
I am afraid to look.

Antony
> I look
At you because my fate has made
Me brave enough to look.

Cleopatra
> I wish
To turn away yet cannot.

Antony
> I do
Not wish to yield and yet I yield.

Cleopatra
You flatter me, yet speak so harshly.

Antony
Your tone of voice, oh lovely queen,
Denies your beauty.

Cleopatra
> I beg you, leave
At once. If you do not, I know
That I shall die.

Antony
> To leave would be
To leave myself behind, and yet
I do as you command.

He starts to leave.

Cleopatra
> No, please!
Please stay! But why do I betray   820
Diana's law of chastity?

Antony
> And why am I the prisoner
> Of love's relentless tyranny?

Cleopatra
> Guards! Seize this man! I am resolved
> That he shall die.

Antony
>   Soldiers! Help me! Put
> An end to Cleopatra!

Sound of drums.

Cleopatra
>   No, stay
> Your swords! To kill him is to kill
> Me too.

Antony
>   No, spare her life. Her life
> Is also mine. Octavian, now
> I understand!

Cleopatra
>   I shall not be
> Love's victim. Mark Antony, you are
> To leave at once.

Antony
>   I cannot, yet
> I must. I shall return to Rome,
> Acknowledging love's victory.

Cleopatra
> No, do not go! I offer you Alexandria.

Antony
> I wish to conquer only Cleopatra.

Cleopatra
> My soul is yours. What am I saying?

Antony

My fate is yours. What am I doing?
I leave at once.

Cleopatra

        As I do too.
You'll not set eyes on me again.   840

Antony

Nor you on me!

Cleopatra

        What doubts are these
Produced by passion?

Antony

          Oh, how can love
Cause such confusion?

Both

         To arms, to arms!
Let battle commence, and love's defeat
Become our mission!

Act Two

Offstage the sound of ships laying anchor.

Octavian (*off*)
　　The water is too shallow. The keel
　　Begins to scrape the sand.

Lepidus (*off*)
　　　　　　　　　　　Cast the line.
　　Let's see how deep it is.

Irene (*off*)
　　　　　　　　　Take in
　　The sails.

Lepidus (*off*)
　　　　　We'll take the boat and make
　　For shore.

Octavian (*off*)
　　　　　Our ships can rest at anchor here.

Irene (*off*)
　　Both sea and wind have favoured us.
　　We have been fortunate.

Enter **Octavian**, **Lepidus** *and* **Irene**.

Irene
　　　　　　　　This is
　　The shore of Alexandria.

Octavian
　　　　　　　　At last
　　On land!

Lepidus
　　　　The gods have looked
　　On us most kindly.

Irene
　　　　　　　The nightingales

Come out to greet us.

Lepidus

The flowers too.
How beautiful it is!

Octavian

Sight and smell
Both flattered by the perfumed brightness of
The lily. Why, even the sun is envious.
See how it courts the rose and offers it
Its light and warmth, but more from jealousy
Than love, for then it burns and withers it,
Destroying its perfect beauty.

Irene

I am reminded of my fate,
For as the sun consumes the rose,   20
So too am I consumed by thoughts
That I have been abandoned by
Mark Antony.

Octavian

As both of you
Recall, we all agreed that if
He'd not return within one year,
Or we'd received no news, either of
His triumph or defeat, the three
Of us would go in search of him.

Lepidus

Indeed, we all agreed on it.

Octavian

One year has passed and still we have no news.
It could be that his ships have been
Destroyed or swallowed by the waves,
Or Cleopatra's left no trace of his defeat.
If he'd defeated her, the news
Of such a victory would by now
Have reached our ears. In any case,

Our ships have finally arrived and I
Propose we start to see
If he is dead or still alive.

Irene
We need to scour these peaks that strive   40
To emulate the stars.

Lepidus
                              These plains
And forests too that stretch before us.

Octavian
Perhaps the mountain will reveal
Some town or village.

Irene
                              The plain
Seems deserted.

Octavian
                    No sign of life.
Let the trumpet sound. Let's see if any man
Or beast responds to it.

The trumpet sounds. They listen.

The only other sound the trumpet's echo,
In imitation of itself.

Irene
The birds alone are startled.

Lepidus
                              Unless
My eyes deceive me, a man!

Irene
Who runs away from us and seeks
The safety of the trees.

Octavian
                    You there!
No need to be afraid! No use,

He will not listen.

Lepidus

We will not harm
You. Stay!

Irene

We beg you! Why run
Away from us?

Octavian

I am Octavian!

Irene

He hears your name, stops and turns,
And now he runs towards us.

Lepidus

His feet move
With the speed of light.

Octavian

Approach!   60
To those who do what he commands,
Octavian can be generous indeed.

Alligator *rushes in.*

Alligator

I kiss your feet, great lord,
And wait upon your generosity.

Octavian

Who would have thought it? Alligator!

Alligator

Miss Irene, Mister Lepidus! This is
Most fortunate! The three of you!
I can't believe it. What are you doing here?

Lepidus

More to the point, what are *you* doing here?

Alligator
I live in Alexandria.

Irene
Then have
You seen Mark Antony?

Alligator
Of course!

Octavian
Where is he, then? What news of him?

Alligator
The usual. Cleopatra overcame him.

Octavian
Is he alive?

Alligator
Most definitely!

Octavian
You are
Quite sure?

Alligator
He'd be much better off
If he were dead.

Octavian
What do you mean?
I'd give my life to see my friend
Alive. And what of Cleopatra? Is she dead?

Alligator
She is.

Octavian
This is most strange!

Alligator
In spite of which
She's very much alive.

Irene (*aside*)
                    This is the worst   80
    That I could hope for!

Octavian (*aside*)
                    For me the best
    Of news!

Lepidus
            Explain yourself. You speak
    In riddles.

Irene
            We want the truth.

Lepidus
    Why you are here.

Octavian
                How it can be
    That Cleopatra's dead yet lives!

Irene
    That Antony's alive yet dead!

Lepidus
    Come now! Tell us! Your story had better be
    Convincing.

Alligator
                All right, all right! I'll tell
    You everything.

Octavian
                From the beginning!

Alligator
    From the very beginning, my lord.
    I came to Egypt with your army,
    I fought as best I could, but in
    The end not even my great sword
    Could leave its mark on Cleopatra.
    Then, later on, Mark Antony arrived.

He did no better either. As soon
As he set eyes on her, he was
Completely dazzled by her looks,
As though he gazed upon the sun,
And, like a piece of wax, was melted by   100
Its heat. He thought he could escape,
Of course, by going back to Rome,
His passions held in check like some
Volcano which seems to be
Extinct but where inside the lava
Boils and bubbles till it finally
Erupts in ash and smoke. So he
Set sail, but almost straight away
Was overtaken by Cleopatra.
You should have seen her ship! Its masts
Were silver, its rigging and its ropes
Of gold, its sails of finest linen.
The prow was brilliantly adorned
With marble and with ebony,
As well as precious stones. As for
The crew, it was made up of more
Than fifty cupids who shot their darts
At breasts they thought that they could pierce,
While in the stern were sirens singing songs
Of love. Oh, what a battle that   120
Turned out to be! Cleopatra on
A throne of gold, her diamonds
As bright as any sun that ever shone,
And waiting for Mark Antony.
I warned him to ignore her, but what
Can you do where women are concerned?
If he'd had any sense, he would have turned
Away, instead of which he went
Towards her, and was lost immediately.
Imagine it! Those soothing choruses
Of love, their gentle rhythm echoed by
The lapping of the waves. And then,
As if by magic, on the shore,

A great long table held aloft
By metal nets so cunningly
Designed that they were very strong
Yet barely visible. As for
The food displayed on them!
A salad dressed with olive-oil,
Fit for the gods, arranged around   140
A great big pearl the like of which
You've never seen and worth a fortune.
Fish too of every kind, and fowl
And fruit so succulent, your mouth
Begins to water with the sight
Of it. And wine to wash it down
That tasted like the nectar of
The gods, and all of it to satisfy
The needs of these two gods of ours,
Mark Antony and Cleopatra.
I can tell you, she soon lost all
Her inhibitions – as often happens,
It's those who seem the most reserved
Who go completely wild. And, seeing her,
The others too thought they would make
The most of it and be again
What they once were. Old women, chaste
For years, remembered pleasures they
Had long forgotten. And widows most
Devoted to their husbands' memory   160
Were quite transformed, their skirts above
Their heads, their chastity abandoned to
The winds. It was a quite fantastic orgy.
Single girls behaved as if
They'd just been married, and wives
As if they were still single, all
Of them consumed by one desire.
They had as their accompaniment
The gentle cooing of the doves,
Whose soft and tender sounds attended on
Their sweaty thrusting. The lily and

The jasmine, symbols both of purity,
Were cast aside, and favour given to
The clinging ivy, in which they saw
Their own embraces mirrored. The law
Was quickly changed – I mean the one
Which said that women should be burned
If they had sex. Cleopatra passed
A different law which said they should
Be burned if they did not.   180
In short, Venus and Bacchus in, Diana out!
And headaches became the fashion – not
Because you didn't want it, but
Because you'd had too much of it.
As for Mark Antony and Cleopatra,
They entered Alexandria, cheered and
Applauded by the people.
You should have seen the way she looked
At him, devoured him from head
To foot, as women always do when they
Are desperate to have a man –
Believe me, I've experienced it!
And poor Mark Antony,
He looked at her as men are wont
To do when they can't wait to get
Their hands upon a girl but haven't done
So yet. In any case, into the palace
They went, the two of them alone,
To see how best to bring about the peace.
It must have been a tricky business,   200
'Cos they've been there a month and not
A sign of them. Quite obviously,
A difficult negotiation!
So that's the way things stand. It's not
So much Mark Antony's dead as your faith
In him! And Cleopatra's not
Dead either: more a case of red-hot desire!

Octavian
Be silent! Do you think I believe

This story? Mark Antony's a friend
To whom I'd trust my life, and I,
Not he, love Cleopatra. He's come
To conquer her on my behalf,
So I can have her for myself.

Alligator
And does he know you love her?

Octavian
                              Of course
He does! The earth, the sea, the heavens,
All know I adore and worship her.

Alligator
Then he's a traitor!

Octavian
                    He is my loyal friend!

Lepidus
It's true, of course, that all is fair
In love and war.

Alligator
                And what I've said
Is also true, sir. Was not Mark Antony   220
Engaged to marry your sister?
Well, now he only wants Cleopatra.

Irene
Be silent! Have you no shame?
I'll have your tongue out!
How dare you suggest that Antony
Betrays me, when I am the sun in his
Bright heaven! He loves me!

Alligator
                        He may do, madam,
But he loves Cleopatra even more.

Irene

You lie!

Alligator

I'll prove it to you.

Irene

Then prove it!

Alligator

My life's in danger.
I've been in hiding for a month,
And just because he heard me say
He was deceiving you with her.

Irene

He threatened your life?

Alligator

He did.

Irene

And does this woman know Mark Antony's
Engaged to me?

Alligator

I doubt it, madam.

Irene

And I doubt too that she loves him.

Alligator

Oh, you shouldn't doubt it.
He's head-over-heels with her and so
Is she with him!   240
If you want to know more . . .

Octavian

You've said enough!

Alligator

Then I'll be off.

Octavian
                    Wait! Where is
    Mark Antony?

Alligator
                    Four miles or so
    From here. He's in this villa by the sea.

Octavian
    Then you must show us where it is.

Alligator
    Follow me, my lord.

Octavian
                            I swear
    By every star that shines . . .

Irene
    By that bright moon which, sister to
    The sun, illuminates the darkest night . . .

Octavian
    That this ungrateful friend shall die!

Irene
    That he who has betrayed my trust
    Shall soon lie in his infamous blood!

Octavian
    Until that is achieved, I shall
    Not rest . . .

Irene
                        Nor I consent to sleep . . .

Octavian
    I shall not satisfy my thirst . . .

Irene
    Nor I the growing pangs of hunger . . .

Octavian
    Until I've drunk his blood . . .

Irene

                              Until
His veins are emptied of their vital substance.

Octavian
Mark Antony shall die!

Irene

                        Must die
For what he's done!

Lepidus

                        Since your cause   260
Is similar, you go by land.
I'll go by sea.

Octavian
                  Embark at once.

Lepidus (*aside*)
At last I take revenge on him
For my offence!

Irene
                  Let the trumpet sound!

Lepidus (*aside*)
With Antony dead, Irene shall be mine!

Exit **Lepidus**.

Octavian
You, lead the way!

Alligator
                  Just as you say,
My lord. I'm at your service.

Exit **Alligator**.

Octavian
                        Irene,
Come.

Irene
> Your revenge is also mine,
Octavian.

Octavian
> He has offended both of us,
We'll see the traitor dead.

Irene
>> Indeed
We shall.

Octavian
> Jealousy and anger are
My spur.

Irene
> Revenge and hatred mine.

Octavian
Our days of friendship are over.

Irene
Let no one put faith in any lover!

They exit. Enter **Lelio** *and* **Cleopatra** *from one side of the stage,* **Mark Antony** *and* **Octavius**, *a captain, from the other.*

Cleopatra
Lelio, leave me!

Lelio
> Your majesty
Should take great care.

Antony
>> Octavius, I wish
To be alone.

Lelio
> Do not allow
Yourself to be deceived by love.

Cleopatra
Please go now, Lelio.

Octavius
                    By doing this,
You will offend Octavian greatly.   280

Lelio
They will deprive you of your kingdom.

Antony
I do not wish to conquer Egypt,
Rather to be ruled by Egypt.

Octavius
                    Am I
To think that you, who worshipped Mars,
Are ruled by love?

Antony
                    I am, Octavius.

Lelio
Must I believe that you, for whom
Disdain became an art, are now
Love's helpless victim?

Cleopatra
                    I am, Lelio.

Octavius
That you are now Octavian's enemy?

Antony
It's true, Octavius.

Lelio
Your subjects will not endure it.

Octavius
Irene will be outraged by it.

Antony
You are saying Cleopatra can't be mine.

Cleopatra
You are implying Antony
Can never be my husband.

Octavius
                        Your soldiers are
Resolved to kill her.

Lelio
                    Your soldiers are
Determined he shall die.

Cleopatra
                    Lelio,
Please leave me.

Antony
                    Octavius, wait outside.

They both leave.

I must control my feelings.

Cleopatra
                        I must
Not let this passion overwhelm me.

Antony
I'll speak to her. My mind's made up.   300

Cleopatra
There is no other way. He must
Be told. Mark Antony, my only love,
Who gives my life true meaning. You know
That, since the day we met,
You have become the master of
My will, have softened that disdain
I felt for other men, have so
Affected everything that I
Believed, that I am like the softest wax
In your hands. That night we spoke
Together in the garden, the whole
Of Nature seemed to inspire love.

The stream appeared to speak to us,
Its gentle sound dismissing my
Anxieties and doubts. Despite
My fears, it made me much more bold,
And you, regardless of my own
Reserve, more confident that I
Would look on you with greater favour.
We were beguiled and lulled by all   320
The sounds that then surrounded us.
I can remember saying to myself:
'The love that is not blind does not
Deserve the name of love.' It was
The moment when my soul became
Infected by that poison we call love.
Your voice, so soft and so persuasive then,
Entranced my ears and made my eyes
Go mad with jealousy that, though
They had the power of sight, they could
Not listen to the magic of
Your voice. My other senses too
Were envious of my ears, each vying with
The other, so that my eyes were ears,
My ears eyes. You told me that you loved
Me more than words can say, and I
Echoed your every word. The one
Thing that we both desired was to
Be married, allowing Hymen to correct
Blind Cupid's folly; but, knowing that,   340
My subjects turn against me now,
And quote our ancient law, which states
That no Egyptian be allowed
To enter into marriage with
A Roman. Because I cannot violate
My country's laws, and, what is more,
Because your life, which is mine too,
Is threatened by a double danger –
Of losing yours and with it mine –
I beg you pay attention to

These tears and leave this place for Rome,
Thus sparing both of us, for in
The knowledge that you live I cannot die.
A plague upon the hunter who
Disturbs the lives of doves who in
The quiet of their nests wish but
To celebrate their love! A curse
Upon the predator who uses all
His skill to set a cunning trap
And in the peaceful forest kills   360
The innocent and unsuspecting deer!
I beg you, Antony, leave at once.
Entrust the winds with your sails,
And if they are not strong enough,
My sighs shall help you on your way
Before my subjects claim your life.

Antony
My dearest Cleopatra!

Cleopatra
                    No!
I will not let you change my mind.
I'd rather tear this blindfold from
My eyes and stop my ears with it.

Antony
Our love is like the rose that buds
In May, enclosed by thorns; that sickens with
The fall of night and does not open with
The day. By those sweet eyes that I
Adore, two goddesses to whom
I sacrifice my life, if this
Were but my only anguish!

Cleopatra
What anguish is there other than
The thought of losing me?

Antony
                    There is

A remedy for that. Leave Egypt.   380
Step down as queen of Alexandria.
Accept instead the throne of Rome,
Which I would place at your feet.
And yet that makes the risk much greater.

Cleopatra
You speak in riddles. I do
Not understand. There is much more
To this than you are telling me.

Antony
Much more.

Cleopatra
                Then tell me!
What risk are you referring to?

Antony
The truth is that Octavian loves you, I
Adore you, I am his closest friend
And he mine. He also placed his faith in me
To conquer you for him, to place you in
His arms. In short, for me to fall in love
With you is to betray my love
For him, though not to fall in love
With you would also be the greater crime.
There is Irene too, Octavian's sister.
She is to be my wife. Imagine, then.
If I persist in loving you,   400
In being dazzled by these eyes,
All those who serve me now will soon
Become my enemies. For you
To come with me to Rome would be
To bring upon myself at one fell swoop
My own destruction. To her I'd seem
A faithless lover, to him
A treacherous friend. To seek
Irene's arms would be to seek
A passion now gone cold; to meet

Octavian a confession of my crime.
Your subjects seek my death,
Offended by my actions, while mine
Seek yours. To cease to love you is
Inconstancy; to die for love
The greatest folly. And yet, to leave
You is to bring about my death,
To stay to die as well. What can
I do in circumstances such
As these, when staying here means losing you,   420
And leaving here means I have lost you?

Cleopatra

You are the vilest and most treacherous
Of men! You are unworthy of
My love, do not deserve to look
Upon the beauty of these eyes!
How dare you now repay
My love with this, and make me feel
Such jealousy and rage as I
Have never felt! I am the goddess of
Men's wills, and all who think they can
Betray me pay for their sins.
You say this woman is to be
Your wife, implying you cannot
Abandon her. That being so,
I pay you now in kind: Octavian shall
Be mine! You say he worships and adores me.
So be it! I'll give him his
Reward, which will in turn become
Your punishment.

Antony

                    But I said my love
For her has now gone cold. Is that
Betrayal of my love for you?   440

Cleopatra

And yet she is to be your wife,
Which means that you have loved her.

Antony

　　But if I say that I adore you,
　　That means that I've forgotten her.

Cleopatra

　　I am the one you must forget.
　　My pride is such, I cannot share
　　You with another woman, however much
　　I feel for you, no matter what
　　You feel for me. I may well burn
　　With jealousy, but I can only treat
　　You coldly now. What else is there to say?

Antony

　　Cleopatra, I loved Irene, yes,
　　But then I had not set eyes on you.
　　The moment I did, I was entranced.
　　To value light, one has to know
　　The dark. If night did not exist,
　　The sun itself would not seem wonderful.
　　Who can appreciate the rose
　　Without having seen the lily first?
　　Who wonders at the mighty sea   460
　　Without having seen the tiny stream?
　　If frosty December had not arrived,
　　How could we be amazed by April?
　　And who would know what virtue is
　　If he had not encountered vice?
　　This being so, if I had not
　　Loved someone else, I could not pass
　　From that dark night to your sun;
　　From that pale lily to your rose;
　　From that small river to your sea;
　　From that December to your spring.
　　In short, when I consider both of you,
　　She is the night, the lily, river, winter,
　　And you the sun, the rose, the sea, the spring.

Cleopatra

　　Then if you have discovered the sun,

Reject dark night.

Antony
I do, I swear it.
I reject Irene. I admit only my love
For you.

Cleopatra
Then I reject Octavian.
He has no hope of me.

Antony
You are
The only woman in my life.   480
What shall we do?

Cleopatra
We'll flee from here,
Our refuge shall be Asia's provinces,
Their mountains our hiding-place,
And you my kingdom.

Antony
I your slave,
Obedient to your will alone.

Cleopatra
We should leave now. The sun,
Exhausted by the labours of
The day, seeks welcome rest. The time
Is opportune, the sea at hand,
Your galley close to shore. Let's make
Our destination distant Asia.

Antony
First let me advise Octavius.
He is a trusted and most loyal man.
He will ensure that my men
Will not attempt to take your life.
Wait for me here.

Cleopatra

From this very day,
You are the north star I shall follow,
The single path I tread. Will you be
My husband?

Antony

Indeed I shall.

Cleopatra

My love is such that I take pleasure in   500
The jealousy I felt. It was
But part of what I feel for you,
And, added to the flames of love,
Made it burn more fiercely.

Antony

I too
Am glad you said you'd love Octavian.
The fear of it guarantees
My own devotion.

Cleopatra

Go, then. I'll wait
For you. But never tell the woman you love
That someone else admires her.
Love is unpredictable.
No woman is so constant that
She does not welcome flattery
From other men. And so, if she
Has cause for jealousy at any time,
She may, to take revenge, reward
Another man who says he loves her,
Simply to punish the one she truly loves.

Antony

I do not doubt your constancy.

Cleopatra

My love for you is proof of it.

Antony
 I'll make arrangements for our swift   520
 Departure.

Cleopatra
                Go carefully. My life
 Is in your hands. Without you I have
 No life.

Antony
                Without you there is only death.

Exit **Mark Antony**.

Cleopatra
 Till he comes back, these laurel trees
 Shall be my hiding-place. But what's
 That sound? I'd best conceal myself
 And pray to heaven it grants me all
 That I desire.

Enter **Octavian**, **Irene** *and* **Alligator**.

Alligator
 Tread quietly, as if you were
 A mouse.

Octavian
                I tread so quietly
 That steps dictated by my anger
 Seem like steps silenced by my fear.

Alligator
 This is the house where Antony
 Spends all his time with Cleopatra.

They advance quietly.

Irene
 I swear revenge upon this most
 Ungrateful villain!

Alligator
                My lord Octavian, come

This way. You too, most beautiful Irene.

Cleopatra
The voice I hear speaks of Octavian, then
Irene. How is it possible
That they are here in Alexandria?   540
What turn of Fortune's wheel is this?

Octavian
Alligator! Was it not here
The beautiful and cruel Cleopatra
Attacked my army?

Alligator
                    It was, sir.

Octavian
                              Then the gods
Shall help me defeat her!

Irene
The moon is hidden by the clouds.
Tell us how best we can attack
The city. My hatred guarantees
Our quick success.

Octavian
                    The walls are just
As lofty as her arrogance.

Alligator
Best follow me, my lords. And careful where
You put your feet. This meadow's full
Of poisonous asps. One bite proves fatal.

Irene
My rage is just as poisonous,
Yet, far from killing me,
It fires my resolve.

Octavian
                    Listen! The sound
Of voices. And in the distance, lights.

Alligator
A day of celebration, sir.
The whole of Alexandria's having fun.
See for yourself, there's music there,   560
And feasting, and dancing and gaming too.
Just look at that old fellow. He must
Be eighty at the very least,
Yet he fancies that girl – sixteen at
The very most. And over there,
That old girl, sir. Her face as wrinkled as
A prune, and yet, as soon as she
Sets eyes on that young boy, she's after him.
The old folk don't think twice in
Alexandria, sir. It's what
You'd call a pensioner's paradise.

Octavian
Be silent! Listen! Someone sings.

Voice (*off*)
Two lovers, one like Venus, one like Mars.
They drink each other's souls
Through their eyes.
Mark Antony's betrayed Octavian.
For where love rules,
It follows there are lies.

Octavian
The song
Confirms his guilt. He'll pay for this
Offence, this sword the sharper still   580
To punish his foul treachery.

Voice (*off*)
He turned his back upon his wife,
Rejecting her most cruelly.
Rejoicing in each other's arms,
Cleopatra and Mark Antony.

Irene
Revenge shall be mine. Who'd have thought

He'd be so cruel? But this I swear:
This man has failed me, this steel will not.

Cleopatra (*aside*)
This song has painted only half the picture.

Octavian
This song has pierced my soul!

Irene
                      Must I
Believe my ears were made for this?

Octavian
Look there! It seems that Lepidus
Attacks her ships.

Irene
               Then I shall scale
The city walls.

Octavian
           Irene, wait.

Fire offstage.

Irene
The sea is all ablaze, the beach
On fire.

Octavian
          Then we'll attack together,
This villa, the city and her ships.

Alligator
I think it's time I put my faith
In my two feet again.

Octavian
              Irene,
Attack the city walls.

Irene
             And you,

                            600

Octavian, burn the villa to the ground.

Octavian
Summon your troops. Let's go.

Alligator
So say all of us! Alligator, go!

Irene
And take revenge on both of them.

They leave.

Cleopatra
                              Both land
And sea are covered with their soldiers.
Oh, where can I find Mark Antony?
The sea is hidden by a pall
Of smoke. Where is my lord and husband?
Our love is but a moth about
To be consumed by flames. And now
Another fire closer still.

Octavian (*off*)
Burn the villa to the ground. No one shall
Be left alive.

Cleopatra
                    Octavian too
Seeks only my defeat. How different things
Would be if I had not rejected him.

Irene (*off*)
I swear that treachery
Shall earn its own reward.

Cleopatra
                              Her troops
Set fire to the city walls.
My instincts tell me Antony
Is either dead, or death is near,   620
And my life at an end. I pray
Irene is the one to find

Him first. I cannot think that she
Will kill him. I must call out, and yet
My voice lacks strength above the sound
Of battle. (*She calls.*) Mark Antony! No point,
He cannot hear me. I'll try
Again. Antony! My lord and husband!

Enter **Antony** *with sword drawn.*

Antony
Such is my love, I leave
The battlefield where I am needed most,
And risk being called a coward. I heard
Her voice call out, its tone so piteous
I came at once. I am resolved
To save her life. My ship is ready to
Depart and take us both to safety.
Cleopatra!

Cleopatra
                    Mark Antony!

They call out simultaneously, so that neither hears the other.

Antony
                                        I thought
I heard my name.

Cleopatra
                                    I swear that someone called
To me.

Antony
            My voice encounters voices on
The wind, only to be drowned by them.

Cleopatra
I'll call once more. Mark Antony!   640

Antony
Cleopatra!

Enter **Lelio** *and* **Octavius** *bearing flaming torches.*

Octavius
Lelio, here!

Cleopatra
Is that my husband?

Antony
Is that you, Cleopatra?

Cleopatra
Lelio!

Antony
Octavius, what are you doing here?

Lelio
You have to come with me.

Octavius
Come with me
At once, my lord.

Antony
If the ship is set
To sail, I am the happiest of men.

Cleopatra
If I can only speak with Antony,
I am the happiest of women.

Octavius
Lepidus has set the ship on fire.
It burns upon the waves.

Lelio *speaks to* **Cleopatra**, **Octavius** *to* **Mark Antony**.

Lelio
If you
Do not return, the city will
Surrender.

Octavius
Your men have need of you,
My lord.

Antony
> We have to help her people.

Cleopatra
No, go and lead your men in battle.

Lelio
Remember, your subjects seek
Mark Antony's death.

Octavius
> Your men would put
An end to Cleopatra.

Cleopatra
> Wherever you are,
I wish to die.

Antony
> And I with you.

Lelio
Ten thousand men all share your anger.

Octavius
Two thousand men would be inspired by   660
Your valour.

Antony
> Then we shall put an end
To it. Irene and Lepidus shall die.

Cleopatra
Octavian dead as well!

Antony
Since you have loved me for my bravery,
I would not have you hate me for
My cowardice.

Cleopatra
> And I, since you
Have loved me in my victories,
Would not have you despise me in

Defeat.

Antony

       Go, then, Cleopatra. Save
Your city.

Cleopatra

       And you, Mark Antony, lead
Your troops in battle.

Antony

               I go in fear.

Cleopatra

Of what are you afraid?

Antony

Of never seeing you again,
Such is our fate.

Cleopatra

           Have faith.
Do not doubt my constancy.

Lelio

Look there! The city wall is broken!

Octavius

My lord! Your soldiers turn their backs
And flee.

Antony

       Then let us take our swords.

Cleopatra

Assist our city!

Antony

          Take care Octavian does
Not find you!

Cleopatra

        Or Irene you!

Antony

                              Let love   680
Grant me this victory!

Cleopatra

                    And one
Day guarantee our happiness!

Antony
May the gods protect you, Cleopatra!

Cleopatra
And keep you safe, Mark Antony!

Act Three

Sounds of war. Cries offstage.

Lepidus (*off*)
  Octavian, death to all of them!

Irene (*off*)
  Find Cleopatra!

Cleopatra (*off*)
            Death to Irene!

Antony (*off*)
  Lepidus too!

Octavian (*off*)
          Mark Antony
  Must not escape!

Irene (*off*)
            The city is
  On fire!

Octavian (*off*)
        You there! Stop!

Alligator (*off*)
                I'm afraid
  I can't, my lord.

Octavian (*off*)
          Are you a coward?

Alligator (*off*)
  My legs are in charge, my lord.
  They command me to run away.

Octavian (*off*)
  Lepidus is defeated.

Enter **Alligator**.

Alligator
I'd help him if I could, but I can't,
You see, because of my leg. I think
I'd better stop and make this wood
My resting-place. I'll be as quiet as
A mouse and watch the fight from here.
What greater pleasure can there be
Than watching others waging war
When you aren't part of it? I'll be
A commentator on what's happening.
And introducing Mark Antony, champion of
The world, and here the challenger, Octavian,   20
Who's in a fierce mood and slinging hooks
And uppercuts not just at Antony
But Cleopatra too. And then
There's Lepidus. He's set the sea
Alight, and made the water boil
Around Mark Antony's ship, while he,
On board, performs the role of cox,
Urging his men to up their rate –
It's a boat-race now, as you can tell!
It makes me want to be with him, to give
Up playing the role of coward and be
Instead a valiant soldier in
His service! Oh, come on, man!
What are you saying? Control
Yourself! A battle's no place for a man
Like me, for if I'm born a coward,
It's what I'm born to, my nature, my
Vocation, and being brave would be
A betrayal of myself, which means
I'd never forgive myself. Hey, look!   40
Irene's entering the city,
And so's Octavian. And there
Goes Cleopatra, making her escape
On horseback! Two furlongs to go
And not another horse in sight!
She's coming to the last, jumps

It cleanly – no she doesn't, the bloody horse
Has fallen, taking her with it!

Enter **Cleopatra**, *stumbling.*

Alligator
Here, your majesty, best on your feet
If you want to escape.

Cleopatra
                                    Who are you?

Alligator
                                                    Oh, just
A man who happened to be waiting here
In case you fell.

Cleopatra
                              My horse tripped in the sand,
Such is my misfortune!

Alligator
                                    Fortunate, then,
You didn't break your neck.

Cleopatra
                                          If only I had!
Oh, may it please the gods that in
This battle Irene is the victor, not
Octavian. Antony despises her.
She can have the city but I shall have
His love. You there!

Alligator
                              Alligator!

Cleopatra
Do you know where Antony is?   60

Alligator
As far as I know, he's all at sea . . .
I mean, on board his ship. I'll take
You to him.

Cleopatra
> Is he victorious? If
He is, it will ease my sorrow.

Alligator
> Consider
Your sorrow eased, madam. He's wrecked
At least a dozen ships commanded by
That idiot Lepidus.

Cleopatra
> I see
Blood everywhere.

Alligator
> Oh, that's because
Your enemies are put to flight,
Their tails between their legs, and no
One dares confront Mark Antony.

Cleopatra
> Then I
Must join him. Perhaps, after all,
The gods are not against us. The victory
Shall be ours.

Alligator
> Wait, your majesty.

Cleopatra
I cannot.

Alligator
> But look! Octavian's troops
Attack again.

Cleopatra
> More reason why
I must depart. He is my life!

Alligator
You can't get through. Irene's men
Have blocked the way.

Cleopatra
> I must.

Alligator
> And in
The process die? Do you think that life's   80
A shirt, that, taken off, can be
So easily put on again?

Cleopatra
Oh, fortune, why so fickle? Why must
You give, if afterwards you take
Away what you have given? Why make
Us feel that you are on our side,
If later on we are deprived
Of what we had?

Antony (*off*)
> I order you:
Do not retreat!

Alligator
> If you insist
On joining him, you have to dodge
Those arrows.

Irene (*off*)
> Cut off Mark Antony's route
To safety!

Cleopatra
> That voice is itself an arrow.
It pierces my heart!

Alligator
> I think
I'll join the fight. I know
I ran away before, but now
I'll have another go. Well, people do change,
You know! Long live Irene and
Octavian!

Exit **Alligator**.

Cleopatra
                    Irene seeks to intercept
Mark Antony upon the shore!
If only I could bring about   100
Her death and make her heart the target for
This arrow!

She fires an arrow.

                    It misses its mark,
Deflected by my rage. The one
I wished to kill survives unhurt.
Instead I see Mark Antony bleeding from
His wounds. The heavens insist on punishing
Me more, one injury upon another.
Irene seeks to kill him.
I'll save him from her sword, but if
He dies, I'll throw myself into the sea.

She is about to exit. **Mark Antony** *enters, bleeding, his sword broken.*

Antony
Cleopatra, wait! The sight of you
Now guarantees my cure. Why be
Alarmed by this when your darts
Have always pierced me?

Cleopatra
You have to know: my soldiers are
Defeated by Octavian.

Antony
                    Irene is
The victor over mine.

Cleopatra
                    Then there
Is nothing we can do. The fates
Conspire against us.

Antony
                    Why does
Not fortune curse instead the peasant who,   120
In harvesting the corn, crushes
The lovely flower?

Cleopatra
                    The man who cuts
The towering elm merely to destroy
Its clinging ivy?

Antony
                    The animal
Which thoughtlessly devours the honeycomb
Ignoring the earnest labours of the bee?

Cleopatra
On my account you are about
To die.

Antony
          You are my life, Cleopatra;
My guiding light. To die on your
Account is my good fortune.

Cleopatra
                         To have
You share my own misfortune is but
To know you also share my love.

Octavian (*off*)
Look for her among the trees.

Irene (*off*)
For him along the shore.

Octavian (*off*)
                    He may
Be hiding in the forest.

Antony
                    We cannot
Escape. We are surrounded.

Cleopatra

       Then from
This rock I'll throw myself into
The sea. I shan't surrender.

Antony

And I, so no one else can take
You in his arms, embrace you in mine   140
So we may die together.

Cleopatra

       The sea shall be
Our monument. Give me your hand!

Antony

I offer you my soul.

Cleopatra

     Quickly, they
Are coming.

They embrace each other. Enter **Irene** *and* **Octavian** *from opposite sides of the stage.* **Irene** *seizes* **Antony**, *and* **Octavian** **Cleopatra**.

Irene

     Octavian, I have the traitor!

Octavian

And I the cruel Cleopatra!

Cleopatra

Release me!

Antony

     One blow comes quickly on
Another! I curse the heavens!

Octavian

        Must beauty such
As yours go hand-in-hand with such
Ingratitude? My fate is in
Your hands, and so it is appropriate

That with this hand I take revenge.

Irene *and* **Octavian** *draw their daggers.*

Irene
You requested my hand, Mark Antony.
With it you now receive your death!

Octavian
A friend who is no friend!

Irene
                    A lover
Who's a traitor!

Octavian
                    Both of them shall die!
But wait, Irene!

Irene
                    Octavian, stay your sword!

Octavian
It is I who am obliged to kill
Mark Antony. He has betrayed me and
Usurped my love.

Irene
                    Worse still, offended mine.

Antony
Both of you may wish to bring about   160
My end, and yet you cannot; for if
I die, it is because it is
My wish, not yours.

Cleopatra
                    If both of you
Would have him dead, let Irene kill him,
Octavian me, for who kills me
Kills him. Our lives are one, as are
Our deaths. What does it matter who
Kills whom?

Octavian

>   It is my fate that you
> Despise me, Cleopatra. Nothing I
> Can do will change your mind.
> But one thing I *can* do is kill
> A friend who proved himself a traitor;
> Who, when I had entrusted him
> With all the secrets of my heart,
> Abused that trust, and, knowing of
> My love for you, took you for himself.
> I cannot take revenge by killing you,
> For that would be to kill myself,
> But killing him is true revenge.
> So he shall die and you shall live: you   180
> An example of the folly of love,
> And he of treachery.

Irene

> Octavian, wait! The man you wish
> To kill is promised to me in marriage.
> You speak of how he has betrayed
> Your trust, yet make no mention of
> The anguish I have felt. As far
> As I'm concerned, Cleopatra is
> The one who has to die, not he.
> For her to know the one she loves
> Still lives, is easily the greater punishment.
> And, more than that, he'll live and be
> Despised by me. Spare him, Octavian!
> For you the satisfaction lies
> Far less in killing him than in
> The people knowing, while he lives,
> What kind of man he is, and knowing too
> What kind of man you are, sparing
> The life of someone who betrayed you.

Antony

> I'd rather kill myself than have   200
> The two of you decide my fate.

An end to this!

Octavian
                    Which means that, not
Content with such vile treachery,
You'd now admit to it with your death!

Cleopatra
What treachery can he be guilty of
In loving me? The fault lies with his fate,
Not with himself.

Octavian
                    He could have tried to love
You less. Instead, he worshipped you
With such excess that others whom
He should have spoken of were banished from
Your ears.

Irene
                    I wish to know, Mark Antony,
Why you should find my beauty so
Inadequate, when previously
You found it quite the opposite?

Antony
The explanation is quite obvious.
Imagine someone blind at birth.
He's told by everyone that in
The sky there is a dazzling sun.
One night his sight returns, he goes
Outside, looks up, and there above
He sees the moon. 'This is the sun,'
He says, 'and quite as beautiful
As I imagined.' But then at dawn
The sun itself appears in all
Its glory, and, though he has been dazzled by
The moon, he now ignores it in
The presence of such beauty as
He's never seen. To that extent
I too was blind, and when my sight

220

Returned, you were the moon, which I
Regarded as the brightest sun.
But then another sun appeared in
My heaven, more perfect still. This does
Not mean that I do not appreciate
The beauty that is yours; rather,
That I am dazzled by this other sun
Which I must worship or go blind.

Irene

Then I shall be the one to blind you,
By putting out your eyes.

Octavian

               Irene, enough!
I have in mind a novel vengeance,   240
A punishment befitting all
Ungrateful lovers. This castle,
Which once belonged to Egypt and now
Is ours . . . we'll put Mark Antony there
And you can be his jailer,
While I hold Cleopatra in
My quarters, to see if I can't make
Her mine, either by persuasion or
By force. As for yourself, you can
Attempt to win Mark Antony's
Affections once again. If he
Does not respond and she rejects
My own attempts to win her love,
Then both of them can die of jealousy,
She knowing that you see and tempt
Him every day, he knowing that
There is no way I'll ever cease
To love her. There is no lover who
Does not have doubts, and so, if you
Are always with Mark Antony,   260
She will be tortured by the thought
That, if he loved you once, that love
Could now be re-awakened.

The same applies to him
Concerning her. Their mutual doubts
And growing lack of trust will be
The source, much more effective than
A real knife, of their suffering,
And in the end, perhaps, of their death.
And even if that does not happen,
At least they'll be denied the chance
Of setting eyes upon each other.
Love has its limits, its rule is not
Infallible. Does not the moon
Change constantly? Can it be said
The sun, as night descends, is what
It was at break of day? The world
Is subject to constant flux. What we
Love now, tomorrow we may hate.
The four of us aren't what we were   280
A year ago. Who would have thought
That I'd be here, trying to win
This woman's love; that you would want
Revenge on Antony; that he'd
Be overcome at the thought of losing her;
And she'd be so dismayed at being kept
Apart from him?

Irene
                    The plan intrigues me.
Mark Antony, to the castle!

Cleopatra
                              Your plan
Will not succeed. If I am not
With Antony, my love for him
Will merely grow.

Octavian
                    You to my quarters.

Antony
You cannot put the fire out

By moving it. Instead you fan
The flames.

Octavian
                    You are guilty of treachery.

Antony
Guilty only of being in love.

Irene
You are my prisoner.

Cleopatra
                    Impossible.
Mark Antony is my jailer. He has
My soul in chains.

Octavian
                    Your good fortune
Has brought you nothing.

Irene
Your chastity has been of no avail.

Antony
What fortune is there greater than   300
True love?

Cleopatra
                What chastity resists
True passion?

Octavian
                    One day you shall be mine.

Cleopatra
Not if I'm his alone.

Irene
                        You'll come with me,
Mark Antony.

Antony
                    I'd rather die than suffer this.

Cleopatra
Farewell, husband.

Octavian
                        Be silent!

Antony
Cleopatra!

Irene
                    Your words are wasted.

Cleopatra
                                    Do
Not doubt my constancy.

Antony
                        Do not
Be jealous on my account.

Irene
                        For your deeds
Revenge is imminent.

Octavian
                        And time
Will tell if you are constant.

Exit **Antony** *and* **Irene** *one side of the stage and* **Octavian** *and* **Cleopatra** *the other.*

Octavius (*off*)
I've seen some cowards in my time,
But never one like you.

Enter **Alligator**.

Alligator
                        Good day to you, sir.
I think you've got the wrong man, sir.

Enter **Octavius**.

Octavius
Do you deny you ran away?

Alligator

> I don't deny it, sir. But not
> Because of any danger. A call
> Of nature, sir, I do assure you.

Octavius

> You'll be telling me next that you've
> Got balls.

Alligator

> Let others confirm it, sir.
> Would you like a demonstration?   320

Octavius

> As far as I'm concerned, actions
> Speak louder than words. From what
> I've seen, you are a mouse, a hare,
> A greyhound, your greatest attribute
> Your feet.

Alligator

> I do admit they are
> Exceptional, sir. Sometimes
> They barely touch the ground. They should
> Have called me Mercury. But look,
> I'll prove it to you, sir. I'll fly.

He runs off. Enter **Lepidus** *and* **Lelio**.

Lepidus

> This is how it must be done.
> There is no other way.

Octavius

> Am I allowed
> To know what you intend?

Lepidus

> You know
> Already how Mark Antony
> Defeated me at sea and how
> In turn he was defeated by Octavian.

You know too that Irene was
The object of my love.

Lelio
                    Decreed
By destiny, my lord.

Lepidus
                And how
For many years she has despised that love,
A rock resisting my every move,   340
Granite in the face of my advances.
Well, now I have decided on
A course of action that, in years
To come, will be remembered for
Its boldness.

Octavius
                You intend to kidnap her?

Lepidus
I do not want her. My love has now
Been tempered by her coldness. Who wants
A woman who preferred another's arms,
Who, if she were my wife, would only think
Of him and all she once enjoyed?

Lelio
So what's your plan?

Lepidus
                To take
Revenge on her and on Octavian;
On her because she mocked my love;
On him because he gave her to
Mark Antony.

Octavius
                So how will you
Effect this plan?

Lepidus

    By freeing both
Mark Antony and Cleopatra.

Octavius

       But how?

Lepidus

The castle where Irene keeps
Mark Antony, imprisoned in the hope
That he'll respond to her persuasion . . .   360
I've sent a soldier there who bears
A message, informing him that I
Will have a ship prepared to sail
And carry him away from here
To some much safer place. I've sent
Him money too, in case he has
To bribe the guards. As well as that,
A note has gone to Cleopatra,
And with it clothes more suited to
A man, with which she can disguise
Herself and make her way down to the shore.

Octavius

But what is your purpose?

Lepidus

      My hope
Is that Irene will not have
The chance to melt the coldness of
Mark Antony, nor Octavian rouse
The passions of Cleopatra.
When he is gone, Irene will
Have knowledge of the hopeless love
I feel for her; Octavian of
The emptiness created by   380
Cleopatra's absence; and I the joy
Of sweet revenge on both of them.

Lelio

Does Cleopatra know you have

Informed Mark Antony?

Lepidus
                          The men
I sent have now returned. They tell
Me both of them have been informed.

Lelio
Do they also know where they can find you?

Lepidus
Indeed. You'll take a hundred soldiers.
Wait for Antony upon the bank
Of that stream there; and you, with just
As many soldiers, wait for Cleopatra.
I'll see the ship's prepared to sail.

Lelio
We'll make sure your orders are
Obeyed.

Octavius
              Your every wish is my command.

Lelio
Egypt will applaud your triumph.

Octavius
                          And Rome
The boldness of your actions.

Lepidus
Such is my vengeance on Irene.

Lelio
Such your vengeance on Octavian.

*Exit all. Enter **Alligator**.*

Alligator
What can I do to keep this secret,
When all I want to do is spit   400
It out and tell the world what I
Have heard? A secret's just like wind.

It's here inside, rumbling away
Like some volcano, bursting to get out.
It's easier to be a thief
Than keep a secret. Easier
To be a coward too, and much safer.
If you run away, at least
You guarantee yourself a longer life,
But if you spill a secret, you
Could shorten it quite easily.
No, I shan't trumpet it. Octavian can
Find out himself. Let the lovers run away
And follow my example. There's nothing to
Compare with making your feet move faster,
Except, that is, a good long sleep,
Which is the next thing I propose.
I'm supposed to be the look-out here,
My eyes wide open. But when it's night,
It makes more sense to keep them shut.   420
I'll lie down here. The sand is nice
And soft, and the lapping of the waves
Upon the shore is just the thing
To form a pleasant background to my snoring.

Cleopatra *appears on top of a rock. She carries a bundle of male clothing.*

Cleopatra
Octavian sleeps and so
I managed to slip out without
Him hearing me. Lepidus has sent
These clothes with which I must disguise myself
In order to escape. How quiet it is!
The wood so dark! The sea that often is
So restless, now so calm! Oh, how
Can I escape? The guards are everywhere.
If I attempt to move, I shall
Be seen. And yet, if I stay here,
Octavian will awaken and put
An end to all my hopes. What can

I do when happiness is almost in
My grasp and yet so far away?

Enter **Octavius**.

Octavius
Alligator's supposed to be
On watch, and yet I'm sure I saw   440
Him make towards the shore. What's
That noise? It sounds like someone snoring.
Alligator!

Alligator
        Who goes there?

Octavius
It's me.

Alligator
       Who's 'me'?

Octavius
            You were sleeping,
Instead of keeping watch.

Alligator
              I *am* on watch!
That's why I'm bloody asking you:
Identify yourself. Friend or foe?
Your name!

Octavius
       Octavius.

Alligator
          Christ! Top brass!

Octavius
You could be shot for being asleep on duty.

Alligator
I wasn't sleeping, sir. Believe
Me, sir. I can see things better lying down.
You know how sharp-eyed alligators are,

Have you ever seen one standing?

Octavius
Get back to your position.

Alligator
                        As fast
As my feet can take me, sir.

Octavius
I'll expect to see you later.

Alligator
Yes, sir. You will, sir.

Both exit.

Cleopatra
Perhaps my fortunes have improved
Once more. I will not wear these clothes.
Instead, I'll use Octavian's name   460
If I am stopped along the way.
While he still sleeps, his name will help
Me to escape. Oh, let him sleep
As he has never slept, so I
May find my happiness!

Exit **Cleopatra**. *Enter* **Mark Antony**.

Antony
The gold has worked its spell.
It is a key that opens up men's hearts,
And so the most impregnable of castles.
Octavius said he would be waiting there
With a hundred men. How dark it is!
No vestige of that golden light
With which the sun bids fond farewell
To fading day. The sea, the wood,
The fields are all enveloped by
Such dark, impenetrable shadows,
As if the world has once again
Returned to chaos. How can I reach

Octavius and his men and not
Be seen by any of the guards?
I'll take this path.   480

Exit **Antony**. *Enter* **Cleopatra**.

Cleopatra
This bitter sea shall be my resting place,
These waves my tomb. My fate is sealed.
I used Octavian's name, as I
Had planned, and managed to deceive two
Of the guards. But when a third asked who
I was . . . I don't know why . . . I meant
To say Octavian but instead
Pronounced the name Mark Antony.
That name is so engraved upon
My mind, I quite forgot the man
I hate, mentioning by accident
The man I love. My hopes and dreams
Seemed so much closer, the two of us
Together once again, I thought
Of nothing else and spoke his name aloud.

Voices (*off*)
Cleopatra's escaped! Search the mountain!
Find her!

Cleopatra
                    Octavian has discovered my
Escape. They all pursue me. I'll try
To deceive them by throwing these
Into the sea . . .

She throws some garments into the sea.

                              . . .and burying this dagger in   500
The sand!

She sticks the knife into the sand.

But they shall hear for themselves.
(*She calls out.*) Let the world proclaim my constancy!

Octavian, you will never have
My love! I die instead! Let the waves
Embrace me! I throw myself into
Their arms, never into yours!

She pretends to leap into the sea but exits quickly.

Octavian (*off*)
Cleopatra tries to drown herself!
Quickly! Stop her!

Enter **Mark Antony**.

Antony
Either my ears deceived me or
I heard the sound of Cleopatra's voice.
If she now tries to drown herself,
It is to prove that only the sea,
In all its vastness, can ever douse
The fires of our passion. But look!
My eyes confirm the truth, adding to
The sum of my misfortunes. Not even
A breeze and yet the ripples spread
Upon the water!

Octavian (*off*)
                    There below! Save her!

Antony
There is no doubt! His words deprive   520
Me of all hope!

Enter **Octavian** *and* **Octavius** *bearing a flaming torch.*

Octavian
The beach! Hurry!

Octavius
                    Everyone!

Antony
The trees shall conceal me.

He conceals himself.

> Now I'll hear
> The news either of my triumph or my death.

Octavian
> See there! Floating on the water!
> Her gown, and the silken band
> She wore around her head, crowning
> Her perfect beauty.

Octavius
> Take the boat! See if we can find her!

Octavian
> Row to where her clothes are floating.
> We can save her still! Leave the torch!

They exit, leaving behind the blazing torch.

Antony
> Oh, who could be unhappier,
> Misfortune heaped upon misfortune!
> The joy I'd found becomes a portent of
> My death, the sea her tomb! Misfortune piled
> Upon misfortune! And yet look there!
> Something floating in the water.
> I must control myself, or else
> My agitation will disturb the waves
> And make the object sink once more.   540
> She might be still alive! Oh, sea,
> Take pity on my love! Still the movement of
> Your waves!

He rushes out. He returns with a garment belonging to **Cleopatra**.

> I was deceived!
> What I believed was her was but
> This clothing that belonged
> To her . . . the only vestige of
> Her beauty left!

Octavian (*off*)
> There is no sign!

Antony

> Their words destroy all hope! The waves
> Possess her, enjoy the happiness
> That once was mine, and I am turned to stone!
> Cleopatra! Your loveliness extinguished!
> Queen of Alexandria, braver
> Than any man, yet in your love
> The tenderest of women! Your beauty
> A withered flower, drowned in this great sea!
> But I shall follow. If life is but
> A living death, then we shall live
> Together beneath these waves. But no!
> I'll die a different way, you beneath
> The waves and I the earth . . . I have   560
> No sword with which to end it . . . only
> My pain, and such a coldness in
> My heart, I feel already dead.
> I'll make my sword the snakes that fill
> The meadow.

He is about to exit when he sees **Cleopatra**'s *knife.*

> But here's a dagger!
> The sand brings forth a blade, as if
> My tears have been transformed to metal.

He picks up the knife.

> Oh, this is joy! The only time
> The heavens have smiled on me,
> Providing the means to my own end.
> Oh, Cleopatra! I kill myself
> So I can live, for if I die
> With you, I start to live again.

He writes in the sand.

> This sand shall be the witness to
> My good fortune, proclaiming that
> My death is but my life: 'Mark Antony
> Now lives.' Sand, sea, sky, cliff,
> Birds and animals who live upon

This shore, bear witness to the love
On whose account Mark Antony,   580
Though dead, lives on!

He plunges the dagger into his heart. Enter **Cleopatra**, *half-naked.*

Cleopatra
They all believe I'm drowned!
I threw a rock, whose splash, together with
The clothes, convinced them. Since then
These trees along the shore have been
My hiding-place. From there I watched
Octavian and his men set out
In boats to try to rescue me.
And then I heard a voice which said,
If I am not deceived: 'Mark Antony lives.'

Irene (*off*)
Mark Antony's escaped! Close off
The roads and paths. Lepidus has found
Him shelter.

Cleopatra
                    Irene's voice! What joy!
These footprints are the proof that he
And those who helped him came this way.
My hopes were withered on the branch
But now revive. And here some letters,
Inscribed upon the sand still wet
From the ebbing tide. It says: 'Mark Antony
Now lives.' Oh, yes! He lives. It says   600
He lives! A second Phoenix, consumed
By the flame of love yet rising from
Its ashes! Oh, this is happiness!
You plants and flowers, share
This moment with me! You cypresses,
Produce, instead of sterile fruit,
Joyful flowers! You birds who prophesy
Misfortune, sing of better things to come!
But there! What's that? On that green slope

Beside the stream that splashes drops
Of water more like pearls upon its banks,
There is a shape . . . I think a body.
Whose blood begins to form a second stream,
Turning the sand bright red. This torch
Will show me who this is and if
He is alive or dead!

She takes the flaming torch from the sand and goes over to the body.

No! No!
This cannot be! This cannot be!
My love, my life, my husband dead!
And with my dagger, turning the jasmine of
Your flesh to bright carnation! You were   620
The sun that poured its warmth and beauty on
The earth, and now your flesh is more
The colour of the moon, eclipsing that sun.
And with my dagger, ending the life
That was my life. Oh, let my grief soften
The stones, my voice break in its own echo!
Let my fate move men and beasts
Alike to tears!

She throws herself on the sand.

The lioness who finds
Her cub bleeding to death and roars
In vain to give it life again . . .
Her grief is mine! I am the broken mirror
In which my eyes no longer see themselves!
My voice sticks in my throat and makes
The sound of some discordant instrument.
Mark Antony, I shall die with you!
We shared one breath. Now we shall share
One tomb. This field is full of flowers,
Which, moving in the breeze, rock to sleep
The poisonous asps. I'll pick one.

She picks a flower and takes from it an asp.

Soothed by such beauty, the serpent sleeps   640
But now begins to stir . . . Pierce my flesh!
Feed on my blood! The woman I condemned
To death, avenge her! Fulfil her curse!
Octavian, Irene, Lepidus, witness my anguish!

Enter **Lepidus**, **Irene**, **Octavian**, **Leilo** *and* **Alligator**.

Octavian
Who is it calls me?

Irene
                        I heard my name!

Cleopatra
Mark Antony is dead! I die with him!

Blood oozes from her breast.

This serpent feeds on my flesh!
Mark Antony was my life and now
My life has been extinguished.
Irene, revenge is yours. But let
The world bear witness to the constancy
Of our love. I die on love's account!
Cypresses, weep! Seas and fountains,
Bring forth your tears, and when
The story of my death is told,
Let people know that 'Here died Antony,
And here Cleopatra.'

She falls across **Antony**'s *body.*

Lepidus
Oh, most unfortunate of lovers!

Irene
He paid the price of his betrayal!

Octavian
The play is ended. Let no one forget   660
This tragic spectacle, nor love's
Uncertainty!

GWYNNE EDWARDS is a lecturer at the University of
Wales, Aberystwyth, and a specialist in Spanish theatre and
cinema. He is the author of a dozen or so books, including
Lorca: The Theatre Beneath the Sand; *Lorca: Living in the Theatre*;
The Discreet Art of Luis Buñuel; *A Companion to Buñuel*; and
Almodóvar: Labyrinths of Passion. He has translated three
volumes of Lorca's plays for Methuen, *Calderón Plays: One*,
Three Spanish Golden Age Plays, and *Contemporary Latin American
Plays*.

Made in the USA
Las Vegas, NV
20 January 2023